P9-CCB-299

STUDENT GUIDE TO ENGLISH COMPOSITION 1001

2016–2018

EDITORS:
JOYCE MALEK, CHRISTOPHER CARTER, RICH SHIVENER, KELLY BLEWETT

UNIVERSITY OF CINCINNATI
McMICKEN COLLEGE OF ARTS AND SCIENCES

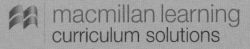
macmillan learning
curriculum solutions

bedford/st.martin's · hayden-mcneil · w.h. freeman · worth publishers

Copyright © 2017 by the Department of English and Comparative Literature, University of Cincinnati, text and photos for both printed and digital editions

Copyright © 2017 by Chloe Hemingway for cover design

Copyright © 2017 by University of Cincinnati, for all student essays in printed and digital editions. All rights reserved.

Copyright © 2017 by The University of Cincinnati for logo use.

Copyright © 2017 by University of Cincinnati for text photos as marked. All rights reserved.

Photos provided by Hayden-McNeil, LLC are owned or used under license

In-text photos provided courtesy of the Archives & Rare Books Library, University of Cincinnati, as marked in printed and digital editions

All rights reserved.

Permission in writing must be obtained from the publisher before any part of this work may be reproduced or transmitted in any form or by any means, electronic or mechanical, including photocopying and recording, or by any information storage or retrieval system.

Printed in the United States of America

10 9 8 7 6 5 4 3 2 1

ISBN 978-0-7380-8242-4

Macmillan Learning Curriculum Solutions
14903 Pilot Drive
Plymouth, MI 48170
www.macmillanlearning.com

Malek 8242-4 F16

Hayden-McNeil Sustainability

Hayden-McNeil's standard paper stock uses a minimum of 30% post-consumer waste. We offer higher % options by request, including a 100% recycled stock. Additionally, Hayden-McNeil Custom Digital provides authors with the opportunity to convert print products to a digital format. Hayden-McNeil is part of a larger sustainability initiative through Macmillan Learning. Visit http://sustainability.macmillan.com to learn more.

TABLE OF CONTENTS

WELCOME TO THE GUIDE   1

UNITS   31

MINI-WORKSHOPS   63

STUDENT WRITING   75

Photo from the *UC Drawn* exhibit from UC's Philip M. Meyers, Jr. Memorial Gallery, 2015.

Credit Chris Carter and Joyce Malek.

Copyright 2017 by Department of English, University of Cincinnati. All rights reserved.

Acknowledgements

The *Student Guide to English Composition 1001* is designed for students taking first-year composition through the McMicken College of Arts and Sciences at UC. This guide is revised every two years and represents the thinking and efforts of many people involved in English Composition: faculty and graduate assistants who regularly teach 1001, members of the 2010–2012 Composition Advisory Committee who revised the course curriculum, and this edition's first-year writers, whose work serves as examples for discussion. The editors wish to acknowledge and thank everyone who has helped shape this edition of the *Guide*!

Thank you to Alan Bothe, Jennifer Lange, and Geri Hinkle-Wesseling for the skilled, patient, and good-humored administrative support they provide to the Department of English and Comparative Literature and to the Composition Program.

Serving as models for imitation and discussion, student essays continue to be an important part of the *Guide*. As usual, selecting essays from among the many we receive is a difficult process, but an exciting one, too, as it gives us a chance to read the writing our students produce in their first-year composition course. We acknowledge and thank the students whose work you'll find in the last section of the *Guide*: Alison Arnone, Tyler Creel, Zac Davis, Matthew Dobrilovec, Thomas Dzierzak, Mattina Girardot, Connor Howard, Greyson Marks, Julia Sharmon, and Hannah Thomas. Thank you also to their instructors: Kelly Blewett, Christiane Boehr, Molly Brayman, Caitlin Doyle, Les Kay, Susan Meier, Sarah Rose Nordgren and Rich Shivener.

Congratulations and thank you to Chloe Hemingway for her winning cover design. We'd also like to acknowledge all of the exceptional student designers who submitted cover designs for consideration; these designers truly made our decision difficult.

We acknowledge the University of Cincinnati Archives and Rare Books Department, especially Kevin Grace, for permissions to feature the historical photos you'll see throughout the guide, and Greg Hand and Doug Nienaber for helping us secure permission. The pictures that appear in this edition acknowledge past and present activism on the campus of the University of Cincinnati, and they exemplify texts as forms of social action.

Lin Fantino and her staff at Hayden-McNeil have published the *Student Guide* since 2007, and we thank them for being such a pleasure to work with! We are grateful for their ongoing professionalism and enthusiasm for our project. Each year, Hayden-McNeil supports our cover design contest with a $500.00 award to the winning designer, and this time around, they awarded $50.00 to each of the students whose essays are featured.

This edition of the *Guide* comes with two options: a free interactive e-book, and for a small fee, a full course platform with the e-book built in. Along with the e-book, you'll find additional recast projects that students created using digital media. We're excited to offer ENGL 1001 students this print/digital package!

The Editors

Mick or Mack, the lion, in front of the original McMicken Hall, circa 1904

Copyright 2017 by Department of English, University of Cincinnati. All rights reserved.

WELCOME TO THE GUIDE
UNITS
MINI-WORKSHOPS
STUDENT WRITING

WELCOME TO THE *GUIDE*

Copyright 2016 by Department of English, University of Cincinnati. All rights reserved.

Welcome to the *Student Guide to English Composition 1001*

The edition of the *Student Guide* you are now reading is the result of hundreds of hours of discussion and contributions over the past several years from faculty who teach in the English Composition Program at the University of Cincinnati. The first *Student Guide to English Composition 101* was published in fall 1999 and was joined the following year by the *Student Guide to English Composition 102*. In 2007, the two *Guides* were combined, and in 2012, the *Guide* changed again as we moved to a new semester-long course, English Composition 1001.

Joyce Malek, Chris Carter, Rich Shivener, and Kelly Blewett, Editors

Copyright 2017 by Department of English, University of Cincinnati. All rights reserved.

Every two years the *Guide* undergoes rethinking, revising, and editing as we strive to define our goals and develop materials that represent the writing and thinking valued throughout the many colleges that make up the University. As we continue to refine our curriculum, we welcome your comments on the *Guide* and how it functions with your assigned readings to develop cohesive instruction in writing.

English Composition 1001 introduces you to the kinds of analytic skills college students are expected to demonstrate as they read and respond to written, spoken, and visual texts. By the end of English Composition 1001, you should be able to analyze and synthesize ideas while remaining aware of rhetorical concepts like audience, purpose, situation, and voice. Over the course of the semester you will also work with diverse Research Steps designed to help you find a topic that engages you, focus your research process, articulate a thesis, and plan out your argument. The writing from your Research Steps will help you compose your Researched Argument essay. After completing your Researched Argument, you will recast your essay into a new form, with a more public audience in mind. You will conclude the term by reflecting on what you have learned about writing and about yourself as a writer, and also analyzing the ways your writing has changed from the beginning of the semester.

What's in the Guide

The *Guide* is divided into several sections. The first three provide information and material related to the composition program and to college-level writing. The Guidelines and Forms section contains information about how your papers will be assessed, grading and editing rubrics, and plagiarism information. Since the writing of students is a critical part of the *Guide*, we include a Publication Consent Form for you to fill out if you would like us to consider any of your papers for publication in the next edition of the *Guide*. The final section introduces you to the Academic Writing Center, a valuable resource for you in ENGL 1001 and your other courses.

The next section of the *Guide* presents the curriculum for English Composition 1001, complete with assignment descriptions and options, goals, and activities that can help you develop your writing. We also include a description of how each assignment fits in to the larger goals and aims of ENGL 1001.

Following the curriculum is a selection of mini-workshops designed to support the reading and writing you'll do throughout the course. The activities in the mini-workshops can be completed during class or assigned for homework and discussion.

The final section of the *Guide* features the most important part of ENGL 1001: student writing. We collect this work to showcase some of our students' best efforts and offer these selections as discussion starters. We know that writing is a recursive art and that every attempt, every draft—even the final ones!—can be altered and improved. We hope that you and your classmates consider how the sample essays and recasts work, how they are constructed to achieve certain effects. Ultimately, we hope you'll apply this analytical and evaluative thinking to your own writing.

This year we're excited to offer once again an online version of the *Guide* in an e-book as a complement to our traditional print version. Recognizing that more and more of our lives seem to happen on our phones or online, we thought a great deal about how best to transition our curriculum to the digital age. We decided ultimately that students and faculty alike gain the most from not having to *choose* between a digital and print guide. As a result, we've given you both! And we've aimed to make the print and digital book look and function similarly, so that you can switch easily between the versions.

In addition, the e-book is housed on a course platform that can be linked to Blackboard or used in place of Blackboard if your instructor chooses. Whether your instructor chooses to use the print version alone, the e-book version, or the full course platform, be sure to visit the e-book version to check out the public Recasts—many of these creative projects can only really be experienced digitally.

We wish you a challenging, successful, and enjoyable experience in ENGL 1001. We hope we've provided you with a valuable tool to complement your instructor's approach to writing. All of us welcome you to the University of Cincinnati's writing program and wish you success in your college career.

The Editors

Sequence and Goals of the English Composition Requirement

English Composition is a university-wide required General Education course, which is designed to help you develop knowledge and skills to achieve the four Baccalaureate Competencies. The Baccalaureate Competencies are the critical abilities shared by all educated persons, and they comprise a major component of the General Education Program. The four Baccalaureate Competencies include: Critical Thinking, Effective Communication, Knowledge Integration, and Social Responsibility. In particular, English Composition focuses on **Critical Thinking** and **Effective Communication**.

Critical Thinking is the ability to analyze, synthesize, and evaluate information and ideas from multiple perspectives. It includes the capability for problem solving, logical argument, the application of scholarly and scientific methods, the accurate use of terminology, and information literacy. Particular critical thinking skills vary from discipline to discipline. **Effective Communication** embraces aural, visual, and language arts, including the ability to read, write, speak, and listen; it is the effective use of various resources and technology for personal and professional communication. The educated individual must be able to understand and convey ideas in diverse contexts, using appropriate communication resources and skills. Among important language capabilities are proper usage, style, and the ability to formulate a coherent, well-supported argument using language appropriate to academic and public discourse.

The English Composition course in which you are enrolled is the first course in a two-part sequence that has been carefully designed to help you develop both critical thinking and effective communication. These competencies are developed and honed over time, which is why we have sequenced these courses in the following manner and why the courses must be taken in order:

COURSE	DESCRIPTION	GOALS
ENGLISH 1001	English Composition 1001 emphasizes critical thinking and persuasive writing skills. Students learn to read critically and analyze a text's content as well as its rhetorical strategies. In addition, students are immersed in research writing practices, learning how to integrate source material into their papers, evaluate sources, and position their ideas in relation to published research. The course aims to develop confident writers who know how to pursue a relevant, consequential line of inquiry.	*After successful completion of English Composition 1001, students should be able to:* • Understand the complexity of different kinds of arguments/issues. • Recognize that different writing situations call for different strategies. • Recognize that texts are in conversation with other texts. • Understand and demonstrate the ethical responsibility of the writer to explore multiple perspectives on a topic. • Understand and demonstrate the ethical responsibility of the writer to cite sources and report findings accurately.
ENGLISH 2089 INTERMEDIATE COMPOSITION	This intermediate, General Education course reinforces what students learn in first-year Composition, introduces higher-level learning about writing and reading, and focuses students' attention on how meaning is made, understood, and communicated across and within discourse communities. The course emphasizes critical reading and writing, advanced research and argumentative skills, and rhetorical sensitivity to differences in academic, professional, and/or public writing.	*Building on skills developed in English Composition 1001, students successfully completing English 2089 should be able to do the following:* • Demonstrate refined rhetorical awareness, including the ability to analyze, compare, and evaluate how rhetorical strategies function within various discourse communities, and to work with a variety of genres to understand how meaning is made, communicated, and debated in various contexts. • Demonstrate critical reading, writing, and thinking skills, including the ability to distinguish among kinds of evidence used in discourse communities, to locate, evaluate, and integrate sources appropriate to research inquiry, and to produce clear, organized texts appropriate to situation, purpose, and audience. • Engage thoughtfully in the writing process, showing the ability to write and revise drafts and integrate feedback into their own writing, as well as critique others' texts. Use flexible strategies for generating, revising, editing, and proofreading, and understand the social dimensions of the writing process. • Demonstrate knowledge of conventions across varying contexts, showing the ability to use conventions of format, organization, and language, as well as appropriate documentation and citation guidelines.

The assignments you complete in the English Composition courses will help you develop transferable skills that will contribute to your development of the Baccalaureate Competencies of critical thinking and effective communication.

English Composition Guiding Principles

We learn to write by writing. Writing competency is cumulative: it takes practice and more practice. Daily writing activities, formal and informal, are crucial to becoming a more fluent, confident writer.

Writing is the content of composition classes. Our goal as teachers is to help you express, in writing, increasingly complex ideas. We value writing that is clear, well organized, rhetorically aware, and critically engaged. These attributes are not specific to composition courses, but are aspects of writing valued across and beyond the academic disciplines.

Writing is a process. Writing courses provide you with opportunities for invention, drafting, editing, revising, and reflection because thoughtful writing requires time and feedback. We recognize, however, that there is no single process that fits every writer; our teachers are attentive to different learning styles and allow for flexibility.

Writing and revision go hand in hand. You will have opportunities for revision in each composition course. Revising requires that writers return to a draft, rethinking and reshaping what it says. We like Joseph Harris's description of revision in his book *Rewriting*: "The aim of revising should not be simply to fix up or refine a text but to develop and extend what it has to say—to make your writing more precise, nuanced, inventive, and surprising" (116). Adding, cutting, moving, rethinking, and reorganizing text—these are important moves for meaningful revision. Editing, or correcting errors and improving sentences for clarity and readability, is an important part of the writing process as well, but if the "big picture" of an essay is not developed, then the sentence-level changes will not make a significant difference to the essay's overall success.

Photo courtesy Archives & Rare Books Library, University of Cincinnati.

Writing happens in a community. UC writing classes provide opportunities for you to share your writing and to read and respond to your classmates' writing. Writing courses are not lectures, but are discussion-based courses that require your involvement and participation. Much of the writing that you do will be addressed to the academic community, which involves using accepted conventions of formal writing, supporting your claim, developing your ideas, and providing context for your audience.

Writing courses teach you how to write well with *and* without teachers. You'll learn how to become better readers of your own writing through teacher instruction and feedback. However, we believe that you are not served well by an approach that places all responsibility for learning on the teacher. Thus, we foster self-confidence in student-writers through activities like peer review, reflection, group work, and the expectation of ongoing revision and research. Our goal is for you to leave our classrooms with a good sense of how to generate ideas for a paper, organize them in a convincing and logical way, integrate relevant research, craft an appropriate voice for an audience and purpose, and revise and edit based on self-assessment and reader feedback.

Writing courses are not grammar courses. Our charge in English Composition is to teach you how to craft cohesive essays of increasing complexity. While grammar competency is an integral component of writing performance, writers do not learn how to write by learning grammar rules. They learn how to write by writing and re-reading and re-writing.

Writing is an adventure! We hope that you'll learn something about yourself through the process of reading, thinking, and writing in our composition courses here at UC. Writing means discovering. Through a variety of tasks and activities, you can explore not only the subject matter of your work, but also your own thinking.

A Note about Revision

What Is Revision?

Revision requires you to work on the thinking, idea development, organization, and overall content of your writing. Revising might mean that you delete parts of or whole pages, add new paragraphs, make substantial changes to ideas in existing parts of your paper, or completely start over. Revision is also simply writing itself: as we begin to fill up a blank page, we constantly tap the backspace button, shifting and changing our words, or searching for a different way to bring a sentence to its end. This is the nature of writing, though you may certainly experience it as difficult and time-consuming. Writing is real work. But, it's rewarding, exciting, and always challenging work that can make a difference in how we understand ourselves and others.

Most writers go through several drafts before considering a piece "finished." When you re-vise, you stand back and reconsider your whole essay, rethinking how its pieces fit together and puzzling through changes that would improve the work overall. In a sense, revision asks that you take a macro and micro view of your work: stepping away from it to get a sense of how your writing is working overall, then examining it closely to make important changes. In addition to improving idea development and organization, we also expect that revisions will reflect careful proofreading and editing.

Our Revision Policy

Our goal is to help you become critical, reflective readers of your writing so that you learn how to engage in meaningful revision on your own. Teacher and peer feedback will help you re-see your essays from a new vantage point. However, revision requires you to do more than make changes based on others' comments—for those comments are always only partial, since readers are not able to identify *everything* that needs to change for a draft to improve. ***Your responsibility as the writer is to learn from your readers by taking their feedback seriously and developing strategies that are based on your own sense of how to better communicate your message.*** To help you develop into a writer who has confidence in your own choices, teachers may stipulate varying revision policies. Nonethe-less, as a program we are unified: revision signifies for us a substantial attempt to rework content and present a refined draft that reflects your best work.

Guidelines and Forms

Overview of Important Dates for Semesters 2016/2017 and 2017/2018

Fall Semester 2016

Classes Begin	Monday, August 22
Holiday: Labor Day	Monday, September 5
Fall Reading Days	Thursday–Friday, October 13–14
Holiday: Veterans Day	Friday, November 11
Holiday: Thanksgiving Weekend	Thursday–Sunday, November 24–27
Classes End	Friday, December 2
Finals Week	Monday–Saturday, December 5–10

Spring Semester 2017

Classes Begin	Monday, January 9
Holiday: Dr. Martin Luther King Jr.'s Birthday	Monday, January 16
Spring Break	Monday–Sunday, March 13–19
Classes End	Friday, April 21
Finals Week	Saturday–Thursday, April 22–27

Fall Semester 2017

Classes Begin	Monday, August 21
Holiday: Labor Day	Monday, September 4
Fall Reading Days	TBD
Holiday: Veterans Day	Friday, November 10
Holiday: Thanksgiving Weekend	Thursday–Sunday, November 23–27
Classes End	Friday, December 1
Finals Week	Monday–Saturday, December 4–9

Spring Semester 2018

Classes Begin	Tuesday, January 8
Holiday: Dr. Martin Luther King Jr.'s Birthday	Monday, January 18
Spring Break	Monday–Sunday, March 12–18
Classes End	Friday, April 20
Finals Week	Saturday–Thursday, April 21–April 26

Grading Rubric

Departmental policy mandates that students must earn at least a C– or better in 1001 before going on to 2089, the next course in the English Composition sequence. Students receive an A for excellent writing, a B for good writing, and a C for average writing. Students who may need more than a semester to write at a passing level receive the grade of NP (Not Proficient). An NP grade is not punitive in that it does not affect a student's GPA; rather, an NP means students must take the course again to ensure that they have the writing skills they need to succeed in future writing tasks. A grade of F is given in cases of academic dishonesty. (Grades in English 2089—*Intermediate Composition, taken the sophomore year, are A through F with no NP.*)

An Essay Is Excellent Because It

- Meets the guidelines and fulfills expectations of the assignment.
- Has a strong focus.
- Demonstrates comprehensive understanding of subject matter.
- Supports ideas fully with relevant reasons, examples, and details.
- Establishes and maintains effective organization.
- Shows careful, probing consideration of audience.
- Demonstrates mastery of sentence mechanics.

An Essay Is Good Because It

- Mostly meets the guidelines and fulfills expectations of the assignment.
- Has a clear, if rather broad, focus.
- Demonstrates competent understanding of subject matter.
- Supports ideas with sufficient completeness.
- Establishes and maintains effective organization.
- Shows moderate consideration of audience.
- Demonstrates solid understanding of sentence mechanics.

An Essay Is Average Because It

- Does not fully fulfill the assignment's guidelines and expectations.
- Has a focus but is predictable or sometimes wanders.
- Demonstrates critical thought but lacks full engagement with subject matter.
- Lacks relevant details and support of ideas.
- Shows occasional weaknesses in organization.
- Shows limited consideration of audience.
- Demonstrates basic understanding of sentence mechanics.

An Essay Is Below Average (NP—Not Proficient) Because It

- Fails to fulfill the assignment's guidelines and expectations.
- Lacks a focus or has one that is overly simplistic.
- Displays clichéd or lackluster writing.
- Demonstrates cursory engagement with subject matter.
- Does not support or develop ideas sufficiently.

- Lacks basic organizational structure.

- Demonstrates little consideration of audience.

- Lacks basic control or understanding of sentence mechanics.

This general writing rubric explains some of the evaluation standards instructors apply to essays. However, students should talk with their instructors about how these standards are interpreted in actual writing samples. Keep in mind that the evaluations or standards students have had in the past do not necessarily apply here at UC. Students should not expect instructors to grade the way high school teachers did. Rather, writers should adapt to the requirements of their present situation and do their best to meet them.

Grade Breakdown

Grades and quality points are as follows:

GRADE	DESCRIPTION	GRADE QUALITY POINTS	100-POINT SCALE
A	Excellent	4.00	100–95
A–		3.67	94–90
B+	Good	3.33	89–87
B		3.00	86–83
B–		2.67	82–80
C+	Average	2.33	79–77
C		2.00	76–73
C–		1.67	72–70
NP	Not Proficient	N/A	
F	Failure	0.00	
W	Withdrawal (Official)	N/A	
UW	Unofficial Withdrawal	0.00	
X	Unofficial Withdrawal—No Participation	0.00	
WX	Official Withdrawal—No Participation	N/A	

Sample Essay Evaluation Form

Name: **Date:**

Title:

	DISTINCTIVE	SATISFACTORY	NEEDS WORK	MISSING
Focus				
• Focus is relevant to assignment				
• Focus is sustained throughout essay				
Development				
• Ideas are thoroughly explained				
• Tone is appropriate for audience and purpose. Alternative perspectives are considered.				
Support				
• A variety of evidence/reasons for opinion are offered				
• Evidence/research is connected to focus				
Organization				
• Each paragraph examines one main idea and contains appropriate reasoning for that idea				
• Ideas are presented in logical pattern with clear transitions				
Mechanics				
• Grammar, spelling, proofreading, sentence clarity				
• Sentence variety and efficiency				

Most of the above categories should be rated satisfactory for the essay to pass.

Responses/Suggestions:

Meets guidelines and fulfills expectations of the assignment ☐ Yes   ☐ No

Explanation of Key Terms on the Evaluation Form

Focus

The focus of an essay is the main claim around which the paper is developed. Say a student decides to write an essay on the topic "spending too much time on the Internet." After giving it more thought, the writer then establishes a focus, e.g., "While the Internet is useful and important to college students, dependence on gaming, social networking, or other Web sites can disrupt a student's daily schedule, impede his communication skills, and even impact his studies." In sum, then, **the focus is the "angle" the writer chooses to take on a particular topic**. Similarly, good or strong writers attempt to present ideas in ways no one else has. An average paper on Internet dependence simply states that it is a problem, while a better paper might argue that students should balance time on e-mail or social networking sites with personal communication, or that schools should provide training on the academic uses of the Internet to help students use the Web for class work. One way, then, to write a good paper is to find a focus that isn't frequently discussed. In short, good writing most often results from thinking about the issue and about how best to express your particular perspective.

Development

One of the challenges of writing is to think through an idea fully and move beyond simply stating your opinion. Developing an idea often involves asking questions and addressing alternative perspectives. Thinking through an idea during the writing process causes us to question our assumptions and, perhaps, change our minds. Your essays should show that you have considered many aspects of an issue. **Simply stating your opinion and moving on isn't sufficient**. Writers develop their ideas by asking themselves a variety of questions, like these: Who has a stake in this issue and why? Who might have an opinion that differs from mine? How would I address such an opinion? An important element of development is how well you address alternative perspectives. Good writers are aware of other people's ideas and how they complement or conflict with their own. If such conflict exists, any essay in which the writer insults or dismisses other viewpoints does not show appropriate consideration for readers and will not be persuasive. Successful writers adopt a respectful stance toward their subject matter and readers.

Support

Remember that every time you write, you try to persuade readers in some fashion. One effective way is to offer support—**reasons and evidence that corroborate, complicate, and develop your ideas**. Support allows you to offer more than just your opinion. There are many kinds of support, including facts, statistics, survey results, personal anecdotes, hypothetical examples, quotes from interviews, ideas from experts and authorities, and so on.

Organization

In paragraphs and in your essay, organization is evident from a clear and logical development necessary and appropriate to the goals of the text. Each sentence should have a main idea, which leads directly to the next sentence. These sentences should combine to form a paragraph with one main purpose. Paragraphs must be linked with clear transition sentences so that your whole paper is unified by a developed, supported focus. Please be aware, however, that this does not happen all at once, and rarely, if ever, happens on a first draft. These links between sentences, paragraphs, and the larger essay often emerge as the piece takes shape.

Mechanics (Sentence Completeness and Variety as well as Grammar and Usage)

Incomplete or confusing sentences, spelling errors, and grammatical errors interfere with your ability to communicate clearly to your audience. Consult your English usage handbook or online resources to learn more about how to avoid and correct errors, and to follow up on feedback your instructor provides.

Class Notes:

Key to Editing Marks

Below are some of the common notations that writing instructors use to alert students to errors. Use the third column to record the page numbers from the *A&B Guide* or other handbook your class is using that refers to the type of error. Use the blank lines at the bottom of the grid to fill in any marks that your professor regularly uses.

EDITING ABBREVIATION	ERROR	PAGE REFERENCE *A&B GUIDE* OR ENGLISH USAGE HANDBOOK
Awk	Awkward	
Cap	Capitalization Error	
Cit	Citation Error	
CS	Comma Splice	
DQ	Dropped Quote	
Form	Formatting Error	
Frag	Fragment	
^	Insert	
Para	Parallelism Error	
Poss	Possessive Error	
P/A	Pronoun/Antecedent Agreement Error	
P	Punctuation Error	
Ref	Faulty, Unclear, or Ambiguous Reference	
R-O	Run-on Sentence	
SP	Spelling	
S/V	Subject/Verb Agreement Error	
WC	Word Choice	

Class Notes:

Plagiarism Explanation and Policy

Plagiarism is using the words or ideas of another without acknowledging and citing the source. The Student Code of Conduct found at http://www.uc.edu/conduct/Code_of_Conduct.html defines "plagiarism" in the following ways:

- Submitting another's published or unpublished work, in whole, in part, or in paraphrase, as one's own without fully and properly crediting the author with footnotes, citations, or bibliographical reference.

- Submitting as one's own original work material obtained from an individual, agency, or the Internet without reference to the person, agency, or Web page as the source of the material.

- Submitting as one's own original work material that has been produced through unacknowledged collaboration with others without release in writing from collaborators.

In addition, the English Composition Program considers plagiarism to include the following:

- Submitting as one's own work, without permission to do so, a paper that was co-authored with another student.

- Submitting an essay that you have already received credit for in another class.

Plagiarism can be purposeful, as in the examples above, or accidental. These examples, though perhaps accidental, are also considered plagiarism:

- Failure to cite quotations, paraphrases, summaries, or borrowed ideas.

- Failure to enclose borrowed language in quotation marks.

- Failure to paraphrase appropriately.

In the English Composition Program, **the penalty for plagiarism, even if it is not intentional, is an automatic grade of F for the course** *and a letter explaining the offense in your college file. Therefore, if you are unsure about whether or not you have cited all of your work properly, ask your teacher before you submit your essay. The following information and your experience in ENGL 1001 will help you learn how to avoid plagiarism.*

Frequently Asked Questions about Plagiarism

How will my teacher find out if I plagiarized?

From the first day of the semester to the last, your teacher becomes increasingly familiar with your writing: your particular style, word choices, syntax, level of complexity, and ability to organize and develop thoughts. If you submit something that departs from your usual writing style, your teacher will likely know. **Plagiarism is a serious offense and teachers do investigate their suspicions.** Keep in mind that if you find an essay on the

Internet, your teacher can, too. In addition, many teachers require students to submit essays to SafeAssign, an online plagiarism detector program available through Blackboard. Protect yourself by always citing any information from any source you've used to develop your essay.

How do I know when to quote and cite?

Quote and cite anything taken directly from another author. Writers primarily do this when the way in which phrases are stated is so memorable, or is so interesting, or so clearly illustrates a point that paraphrasing the information would not serve the intended purpose. Quotations should be used strategically to illustrate and support your ideas, not stand in for them.

How do I know when to cite even if I don't quote?

When the material is not universally known, you need to let the reader know where you discovered this information. If most people already know the information or could find it easily and quickly, you don't need to cite the material. When in doubt, cite your information but consider the following examples:

George Washington was the first President of the United States.

NO CITATION NEEDED

Some scientists credit the Ponzo illusion, first identified by Mario Ponzo in 1913, to clarify illusions regarding receding parallel lines, to help us understand why the moon sometimes appears larger at the horizon than it does when higher in the sky.

CITATION NEEDED

Happiness is something that many people exhibit by smiling, whereas sadness is often, though not always, reflected in a frown or even tears.

NO CITATION NEEDED

The first astronaut to step foot on the moon was Neil Armstrong.

NO CITATION NEEDED

Sjogren's syndrome is an auto-immune rheumatic disease that often goes undiagnosed. Among other symptoms, it can interrupt the ability of glands to produce moisture, thus causing those afflicted to experience extremely dry membranes, including the inability to produce tears.

CITATION NEEDED

Robert Frost's poem "Birches" reflects the tension between restraint and the unleashing of the imagination.

CITATION if this is the opinion of another author but NO CITATION if this is your own opinion

If you are unsure whether or not to cite information, consult your instructor.

A good rule of thumb is "when in doubt, cite."

Ways to Avoid Plagiarism

* **Take meticulous notes.** Whenever you conduct research that references the work of others, be sure to note the following: author's name (spelled correctly); the publication information of the book, magazine, newspaper, Internet site, etc., including the title, publication date, page numbers, and complete Web address.

* **Put direct quotes—anything you copy down word for word—in quotation marks immediately** so you do not confuse them with your own notes. If you take notes carefully and conscientiously throughout your drafting and writing process, you will run less risk of plagiarizing.

* **Be sure you understand your research materials fully.** Without looking at the material, try to put into your own words what you have learned from your research. When you finish, check back to confirm the information. Make sure you didn't unconsciously "borrow" any specific phrases of the author.

* **Use the MLA citation instructions** in the *Allyn & Bacon Guide to Writing, Concise Edition* to make sure you have cited everything properly (Chapter 15, pp. 359–366). You can also consult other reliable online sources such as the Purdue Online Writing Lab (OWL) and UC Libraries Help page for students.

Publication Consent Form
University of Cincinnati English Composition Program

Date: _____

Dear Students,

The English Composition Program is always looking for exemplary student writing that we can publish in the next *Student Guide.*

We are asking for your permission to copy, keep, and perhaps use as examples the work you have completed this semester. In return for your permission, we promise to remove your name and any other identifying information from the material before it is published, if you wish to remain anonymous.

If you are willing to give this permission, please sign the form at the bottom of this page and return it to your teacher with the relevant essays. There are no negative consequences for not giving permission; we completely understand that your work belongs to you.

Thank you for taking this request seriously.

Sincerely,

The English Composition Program

AWC
Academic Writing Center

- ✂ - - - - - - -

University of Cincinnati English Composition Program

Publication Consent Form

I _____ (print your name) hereby grant the University of Cincinnati English Composition Program permission to copy and publish—for the purposes of teaching and research—any drafts, revisions, and memos related to my writing. This includes publication in print and digital mediums.

I understand that my name and any other identifying information will be included unless I wish that information to be removed. I **do/do not** (circle one) wish to remain anonymous.

Signature: _____ Date: _____

Teacher's Name: _____ M#:_____

Email Address: _____

The Academic Writing Center

What We Are

The Academic Writing Center (AWC) specializes in providing writing assistance in all courses, so students can become better college writers. An extension of the Learning Assistance Center, our helpful staff of writing tutors can help you improve your writing, leading to better grades throughout your college experience.

Location and Hours

We are located in Langsam 401N. Our hours are Monday–Thursday, 9:00 a.m.–8:00 p.m., and Friday, 9:00 a.m.–5:00 p.m. (hours may vary during the summer semester). You can schedule an appointment for writing assistance at the center or by calling us at (513) 556-3912 or making an appointment online at lacscheduling.uc.edu. Also, Monday–Friday, 10:00 a.m.–4:00 p.m., we offer drop-in tutoring where students can walk into the center and receive tutoring without an appointment.

Our Services

Our primary service consists of one-on-one tutoring sessions. During these sessions, our tutors will work with you to improve both your assignment and your understanding of the writing process. Some of the things we cover are brainstorming, paragraph development, thesis construction, organization, and formatting. We do not provide editing or proofreading services, but we will be happy to address mechanical and grammatical questions during the tutoring session.

When You Visit

Please bring a copy of the assignment, any additional texts pertaining to the assignment, and writing tools. We also encourage you to bring a working draft of the assignment (unless you need help brainstorming). To ensure that you see a tutor, make your first appointment early in the semester; students who wait until the last minute sometimes find that the schedule is full.

Online Tutoring

In addition to face-to-face tutoring, we also offer online writing assistance. By logging into etutoring.org, you can submit drafts of your writing assignments. Within 48 hours, you will receive helpful points of feedback that you can use to improve your paper.

24

Web Site Information

To learn more about the AWC, you can go to our Web site at www.uc.edu/awc. Through our Web site, you can access AWC information, schedule an appointment, and download helpful writing resources.

About Our Staff

Our staff consists of graduate students from numerous academic departments and undergraduate students who took a semester-long course in tutoring pedagogy. If you are an undergraduate who is interested in working for the AWC, consider taking English 3005: Writing Pedagogy for Peer Tutors. If you have questions about the course or anything else related to the AWC, contact AWC Coordinator Joseph Cunningham at (513) 556-2866 or joseph.cunningham@uc.edu.

Copyright 2017 by Department of English, University of Cincinnati. All rights reserved.

Course Requirements, Goals, and Policies

Instructor: _____

Office location: _____

Office hours: _____

Instructor e-mail: _____

Instructor phone: _____

Course and section #: 15-ENGL-1001-_____

Course time and location: _____

Mailbox: McMicken 241 (8:00 a.m.–5:00 p.m., M–F)

Office phone: _____

English Comp Office: 556-6173 (8:00 a.m.–5:00 p.m., M–F)

Required Texts

Malek, Joyce, Christopher Carter, Rich Shivener, and Kelly Blewett, eds. *Student Guide to English Composition 1001, 2016–2018*. Plymouth, MI: Hayden-McNeil, 2017.

Ramage, John D., John C. Bean, and June Johnson. *The Allyn & Bacon Guide to Writing: The Concise 7th Edition*. New York: Pearson-Longman, 2015.

Texts or Reader chosen by your instructor.

Course Goals

- To improve your critical thinking abilities, and therefore your ability to develop complex yet clearly stated written arguments and analyses.
- To introduce you to the composing process and the notion of rhetorical context, and to help you develop strategies for invention and revision.
- To teach you how to develop an appropriate research project, discover and read sources, and write convincingly and persuasively on that subject.
- To encourage you to read and write more carefully now and throughout college and your career.

Course Requirements

Attendance

You will learn by doing; much of your time in class will be spent in activities, not lectures. It is important, therefore, that you come to class regularly and that you participate in class activities. If you miss more than one week's worth of classes—for any reason, **including illness**—you may be asked to withdraw. Only religious holidays, military service, and University-sponsored events qualify as "excused" absences. If you miss a class, **it is your responsibility** to find out what you missed.

Conferences

Your instructor may require conferences during the semester to discuss your writing. Even if conferences are not required, most students find that talking with their instructors outside of class can be a helpful supplement to class time. Please check your instructor's office hours or set up an appointment as necessary.

Essays

English Composition 1001 begins by examining how texts are constructed to achieve certain effects. The first assignment introduces you to the concept of rhetoric and the strategy of analysis. The second part of the course focuses on the development of a research project. The project progresses from a series of research steps, resulting in a lengthy argument essay that is then recast into a different genre directed toward a public audience.

Your instructor may ask that you assemble a portfolio so you can see the progress you have made from one assignment to another since each assignment builds on the ones before it, strengthening and developing your skills as a writer.

Peer Review

During the drafting and revising process, your instructor will periodically ask you to exchange copies of your drafts with your peers. To make the most of peer review, you should bring in the strongest draft you can produce in the time frame and comment thoughtfully and completely on the work of your peers. After receiving feedback, you will be expected to consider your peers' comments and integrate the changes where necessary.

Research Steps

Before beginning the research paper, you will complete several shorter assignments designed to address the various phases of the research process. Your teacher will determine the number, type, and due dates of these assignments and explain the necessary length and format for each.

Informal Writing

To help you read carefully, your teacher may also ask you to respond in a variety of ways to the texts you read for class. In these responses, teachers are primarily concerned with your effort to think deeply about the assigned topics. Your teacher will explain how these assignments will be evaluated.

Course Policies and Grading

What constitutes a passing essay in ENG 1001?

The evaluation criteria for papers are outlined in the Guidelines section. Essays in English Composition 1001 earn grades in the A, B, or C range. Essays earning less than a C– receive an NP. In order to receive at least a C– an essay must:

- Have a focus.
- Show development of ideas with support for claims.
- Exhibit an organizational strategy.
- Meet the length requirement.
- Be properly formatted and sufficiently proofread and edited.

IMPORTANT: These are minimum requirements for a C–. To receive a higher mark, you must go above and beyond these requirements. Please see the grading rubric and explanation for further guidance.

Course Grades

In addition to individual essay grades, the following grade breakdown illustrates that your class work and daily assignments impact your final grade in a significant way and should be given the appropriate consideration.

Your instructor will direct you on how to fill in the following grade breakdown:

Texts in Action	_____%	Informal Writing	_____%
Research Steps	_____%	Peer Review Work	_____%
Researched Argument Essay	_____%	Attendance and Participation	_____%
Recast Project	_____%		

Possible course grades include A, A–, B+, B, B–, C+, C, C–, NP (Not Proficient), W (Withdrawal), UW (Unofficial Withdrawal), X (Unofficial Withdrawal–No Participation), and WX (Official Withdrawal–No Participation).

Grade Explanation

At the end of the semester, students who have not attained at least a C–, indicating that they are ready for the next course, are assigned the grade of NP, signifying "not proficient." An NP is not a punitive grade (it does not affect your grade point average as an F would); however, it also does not allow you to enroll in English 2089. **If you receive an NP (Not Proficient) as your final course grade, you must retake English Composition 1001.**

For more information on possible course grades like the W, UW, X, and WX, see the UC Registrar's Web site.

Plagiarism

In the English Composition Program, the penalty for plagiarism, even if it is not intentional, is an **automatic grade of F for the course** and a letter detailing your plagiarism in your college file. Therefore, if you are unsure about whether or not you have cited all of your work properly, ask your teacher before you submit your essay. The information in the Plagiarism Explanation and Policy will help you learn how to avoid plagiarism. Please also see pp. 569–73 in *A&B*.

Final Notes

1. The *A&S Faculty Handbook* states that students are to behave with civility and appropriate etiquette toward faculty and one another. Noncompliance may lead to disciplinary action as outlined in the *Student Code of Conduct.*

2. Students with disabilities or impairments that will affect their performance or attendance in the course should present their teacher with official documentation from the Disability Services Office during the first two weeks of class so that accommodations can be arranged if necessary.

3. Because teachers make different arrangements regarding grade percentages and revisions, your teacher will explain his or her particular policies in these areas.

4. One of the best ways to help students improve their writing is using examples from class. For this reason, your teacher may be using your writing—without your name attached—in class activities. *If you are strongly opposed to this in general or for specific writing, be sure to mention it to your instructor.*

5. Because technology is not always reliable, and your instructor may ask you to submit in-process drafts with your essays, make sure you keep copies of all of the work you do for this class, storing them in a safe place in case you have computer difficulty. Keep any work returned with instructor or peer comments—informal writing, peer review drafts, process work, and revisions. Hold on to this work until the end of the semester. Doing so will guard against any unforeseen emergencies (stolen or misplaced essays, faulty hard drives, and viruses).

6. In the University, we regularly communicate using e-mail, Blackboard, and other technological tools. Your instructor will inform you of the preferred method of communication; it is your responsibility to check regularly the preferred tool to receive updates and notices about your class.

7. Begin your work early enough to allow plenty of time for revision. Each essay should be revised for content, organization, and grammar. Proofread and edit your work, and consider having at least one other person review it.

8. Because essays in ENGL 1001 undergo revision, some instructors don't assign grades to individual drafts, while others assign a grade with the understanding that the grade is meant as a marker for the work in progress. Any grade an instructor assigns to an individual essay, prior to the final draft of your work, should be used to gauge your progress and need for improvement in the course. This practice gives you the chance to produce the best work you can for your graded evaluation at the end of semester. If you want to know more about how you are doing in the course, we suggest you track the evaluative marks you receive on your informal writing assignments, peer reviews, and class work, which also make up part of your grade. We also suggest that you communicate often with your instructor about your progress.

9. If you stop attending class but do not officially drop the course from your schedule, you will be assigned the grade of UW (Unofficial Withdrawal). This UW factors into your grade point average as 0.0 quality points (the equivalent of an F).

10. Your final grade in English Composition 1001 is determined by several factors, including your final writing, in-class work, informal writing responses, and participation and attendance. If your final work does not pass, you must retake the course. However, because your final grade takes other activities into consideration, it is possible to have a passing portfolio and still not pass the class because of deficiencies in other areas such as participation and attendance. If you have questions about the Composition Program's minimum standards to pass, see your instructor.

Suggested Weekly Schedule of Assignments Due

These dates are meant as guidelines. Consult your instructor for due dates and detailed unit and daily assignments.

Week 1   Writing Inventory: Fill in column one

Mini-workshops: How I Write; How I Read

Week 2   Submit "Texts in Action" Draft

Week 3   Mini-workshop: Context

Week 4   Submit Researched Argument Step(s)

Week 5	Submit Researched Argument Step(s); submit final draft of Texts in Action assignment
Week 6	Submit Researched Argument Step(s)
Week 7	Submit Researched Argument Proposal or Mini-workshop: Voice
	Writing Inventory: Fill in column two
Week 8	Conferences with Instructor (Weeks 7 and 8)
Week 9	Submit Researched Argument Essay Draft
Week 10	Mini-workshop: Style
Week 11	Mini-workshop: Voice or Mini-workshop: Genre
Week 12	Submit or Present Recast Project
Week 13	
Week 14	Writing Inventory: Fill in column three
	Submit Researched Argument Portfolio, if applicable, and Reflection
	Complete Online CourseEval

WELCOME TO THE GUIDE
UNITS
MINI-WORKSHOPS
STUDENT WRITING

32

PEACE FOR

7 0

NOV. 12
 CONCERT * FIELDHOUSE 8 P.M.
NOV. 13
 STREET DANCE * BRODIE PLAZA
 6:30 - 9:30 P.M. * BEER
NOV. 14
 PARADE 10 A.M.
 GAME 1:30 P.M. - UC vs LOUISVILLE
 DANCE 9 to 1 A.M.
 PRESIDENT'S MOTOR INN
 NEW LIME * Di'Talians
 MUSIC HALL
 HEYWOODS
 BIG RED & COMANCHEROS

HOMEC MING

Used courtesy of the Archives & Rare Books Library, University of Cincinnati. All rights reserved.

UNIT 1

TEXTS IN ACTION

Paint-in for Peace, Vietnam War protest, 1969.

Used courtesy of the Archives & Rare Books Library, University of Cincinnati. All rights reserved.

KEY ASSIGNMENT
Write an essay in which you analyze how texts influence behavior and beliefs.

PURPOSE
Unit 1 seeks to develop your understanding of how language is used to influence beliefs, attitudes, and behaviors. The Texts in Action assignment asks you to examine how and why a text is put together and what effects its rhetorical components have on an audience. By understanding and employing rhetoric, you will be equipped to engage with texts of all sorts, both within and beyond college.

Goals
- Develop and sustain an idea through a well-organized, thesis-driven essay, supported with relevant evidence and examples.

- Recognize the power of language to influence public or private action.

- Understand that rhetorical strategies are deliberate choices used to motivate people.

- Apply knowledge of rhetorical strategies to writing.

- Understand how writers craft arguments to persuade different audiences.

- Demonstrate sentence-level control, including syntax and grammar competency, and cite source material using standard academic conventions.

FORMAT

1200–1550 words (4–5 pages), MLA format

ASSIGNMENT DESCRIPTION

This assignment asks that you explore how a text is designed to affect its audience in certain ways. Think of your analysis as a behind-the-scenes exploration of a writer's or designer's rhetorical choices. Your essay will employ specific evidence from the text you have chosen to study. These may include analysis of tone, sources, visual elements, rhetorical appeals, organization, and genre.

As you try to understand how your chosen text works you might consider the following questions:

- Who are the audiences for this text—who was meant to read it? What specific features of the text help you figure this out?

- What kinds of conversations and concerns are already circulating in the text's targeted audience?

- How does the text fit into those conversations? How does it echo or challenge a community's values?

- How does the author demonstrate authority?

- What kinds of assumptions does the writer make about the audience's values, identities, community memberships? Is the author successful at addressing them?

- What is the author's purpose? What are the desired outcomes or results?

Options

1. Analyze a persuasive visual or written text. What is the context and purpose of the text? What strategies are used to influence the attitudes, actions, or beliefs of the intended audience? If applicable, how has the passage of time affected the text's persuasiveness or altered its original effects? (You may need to research the reception of your text to answer questions about how present interpretations differ from earlier ones.)

2. Analyze a print or visual text by focusing on how genre is central to its persuasive power. Examine how genre interacts with the kind of action, behavior, and/or beliefs that the text encourages. What difference does genre make to the text's persuasiveness?

3. Analyze one section or aspect of the UC Web site. Who is the audience? What is the purpose of this section or aspect of the site? How does the university brand itself? How

---

A&B REFERENCES: HOW MESSAGES PERSUADE

Recognizing the Angle of Vision in a Text, pp. 43–47

Visual Rhetoric, pp. 57–63

Multimodal Texts, pp. 66–70

Image Analysis of Photographs, pp. 146–154

Image Analysis of Advertisements, pp.158–165

does the site use language, images, testimonials, data, and other elements to influence the beliefs and actions of its audience?

4. Analyze a variety of public texts with a shared topic. How are audiences envisioned in these texts? How can the reader identify the intended audience for each text? What clues establish how readers/viewers are expected to act in response to the texts?

5. Interview members or employees who write for a local organization to find out how they use persuasion to incite action. Collect examples of written or visual material produced by and in response to the organization. Consider what the interviews and materials reveal about the purpose and function of the organization.

> **A&B REFERENCES: WRITING**
>
> Messages Persuade through Appeals to Logos, Ethos, and Pathos, pp. 48–50
>
> Creating a Voice Matched to Your Purpose, Audience, and Genre, pp. 55–57

ACTIVITIES: COMPOSE REVISE REFLECT

a. Use your confusion! Identify elements in the text that seem unusual to you. Rather than letting yourself be drawn to what you recognize and understand, seek out unfamiliar words, phrases, arrangements, images, and ideas. Where is the text unconventional or even strange? Chances are, these moments in the text signal deliberate rhetorical choices the author is making to affect the audience's response. Make a list of these aspects and use them as a resource when formulating your analysis.

b. Copy and paste your introduction and conclusion in a new document and read them. Do the two together show that you traveled somewhere in the course of your paper? In other words, do you get to any new insights or realizations by the end of the paper, or do you echo your beginning points? If you have repeated an idea or point, what is useful or advantageous about this use of repetition? Use the insights you gain from this experiment to guide revision.

    Try a similar exercise with a partner. Trade papers and read only each other's introduction and conclusion. Then attempt to explain what you can infer about the paper as a whole. Notice how accurate your partner's assumptions were. Use the insights you gain to guide revision.

c. Reread your draft and write an informal reflection with these questions in mind: What single aspect of writing this paper was the most challenging? How did you approach that challenge? Don't consult your paper as you write; strive, instead, to put your ideas into everyday language, as if you're describing your paper-writing process to a friend. Use your reflective insights for revision.

d. Reflect on your writing process for this essay. How was the experience of writing it similar to or different from other essays you've written? Did you try any new drafting strategies that either succeeded or failed? Do you see yourself falling back on any bad habits or are you discovering new ways to write and revise?

e. One way to analyze the meaning and function of a written work is to use a strategy called "Descriptive Outline" or "Says/Does." To perform a "Says/Does" analysis, read through an essay, writing a "says" statement and a "does" statement for each paragraph (either in the margin or in the table provided on the following page). A "says" statement is a very **brief** summary of the paragraph's main idea. It captures the meaning or message of a paragraph. A "does" statement **describes the function of a paragraph**—what work it does. "Does" statements use words like "introduces," "provides evidence," "presents opposing viewpoint," "accommodates opposing viewpoint," or "refutes." See pp. 102–103 in the ***Concise A&B*** for a discussion of the differences between descriptions of what a paragraph says and what it does rhetorically.

In addition to using "Says/Does" to get at the meaning and function of paragraphs in a reading, you can also apply "Says/Does" to your own writing.

Read **Michael Pollan's** essay **"Why Bother?"** in ***Concise A&B*** **pp. 114–119**, and construct "Says/Does" statements for each paragraph. On the following page, the first three paragraphs (¶) are done for you to provide a sense of how "Says/Does" can work. We've provided spaces for you to consider eight paragraphs, but you can certainly map out the whole text. Try applying Says/Does to your own "Texts in Action." Patterns in the "Does" column may give you ideas for a thesis.

	SAYS	DOES
¶1	There is a troubling disparity between the reality of climate change and what we're being asked to do about it.	This paragraph builds an audience of like-minded readers (through inclusive phrases like "us," "individuals hoping to do something about climate change," "we"); it creates a personal and accessible tone; it provokes with a central question ("Why bother?") that the reader will be asked to struggle with.
¶2	One part of "why bother" is the question of what one individual can hope to do about climate change.	This paragraph questions the idea of a single person working against climate change through an imagined anecdote/scenario and a straightforward, and kind of sarcastic, tone.
¶3	There is a sense that acting individually on climate change is suspicious or invalid.	This paragraph uses a series of strong rhetorical questions to highlight absurdity.
¶4		
¶5		
¶6		
¶7		
¶8		

38

UNIT 2

MAKING A CLAIM

Photo from the UC *Drawn* exhibit from UC's Philip M. Meyers, Jr. Memorial Gallery, 2015. Credit Chris Carter and Joyce Malek. Copyright 2017 by Department of English, University of Cincinnati. All rights reserved.

▓ INTRODUCTION

This unit has two parts: 1) a series of research steps designed to prepare you to write a research-based argument essay, and 2) the researched argument essay itself.

Because engaging in professional discussion is central to success in any field, you will position yourself in relation to relevant and timely conversations around a topic and contribute your own informed perspective to them.

The research steps in Part One will help you explore, expand, reconsider, and reflect on the various conversations that surround current and compelling questions or problems.

Part Two, the researched argument essay, will bring together many of the skills you have been developing throughout the course—close reading, balancing and documenting sources, developing a thesis or claim, and choosing appropriate language and rhetorical strategies to make your case.

Part One: Research Steps

PURPOSE
Part One of Unit 2 provides the framework for an in-depth, research-based argument. The activities in this part of the unit are a series of research steps designed to prepare you to successfully write the researched argument essay.

FORMAT
Your instructor will determine format and steps you will complete.

ASSIGNMENT DESCRIPTION

Your task is to explore, discover, and engage with an academic, cultural, or professional conversation or problem through one or more research and writing steps selected by your instructor. These steps are designed to guide you toward developing a clear and focused research question and hypothesis for your final researched argument paper in Part Two of this unit. Asking clear and focused questions is crucial in the development of an effective argument that has relevance both to you and your readers. Good questions lead to projects that present valuable, informed insights about a given topic.

Goals

* Learn how to ask researchable questions that have complexity and that engage you as a thinker, reader, and writer.

* Emphasize discovery as generative for writing an effective, informed, and timely researched argument.

* Prepare for the thinking, writing, and researching necessary to write a researched argument.

* Familiarize yourself with research conventions and methods for finding relevant source material.

* Explore multiple research genres (i.e., annotated bibliography, proposal, presentation) and their differing purposes and rationales.

* Learn how to initiate, sustain, and complete an extended research project.

Steps

A. **Determining a Research Topic**

B. **Understanding and Using Sources for Discovery**

   Finding and Evaluating Library and Internet Sources

   Exploratory Narrative

   Developing an Annotated Bibliography

C. **Entering the Conversation**

   Creating a Dialogue

   Acknowledging Oppositions

   Metaphor or Extended Analogy

   Thought Letter

   The Five Ws and One H

   Cubing

What Else?

Conducting an Interview

Constructing a Questionnaire

D. Determining a Focus and Mapping a Plan

Moving from Topic to Plan

Considering a Thesis

Mapping Your Ideas

Outlining an Argument

E. Proposing Your Research Project

Drafting Your Research Proposal

Presenting Your Research Proposal

A. Determining a Research Topic

Choosing a research topic can be a challenge. Your topic must be arguable, have scholarly value, contain diverse points of view, and it should allow you to enter and add to a conversation. Because it needs to be manageable, your topic should also be narrow enough for a focused discussion on the topic.

List three topics that you are interested in exploring further and answer the following questions about each:

- What do you "know" about this topic?

- How did you develop an understanding of the topic?

- What is your position on this topic?

- What are the central questions that need to be addressed in relation to this topic?

- What are (or do you suppose) would be at least two important objections to your position on the topic?

- How does this issue relate to your life—your major, career, etc.?

Once you have answered the above questions about your topics, you can begin to narrow your ideas down to a single topic.

▶ *For more information on generating and exploring ideas, see* Concise A&B *pp. 125–26 and 225–26.*

B. Understanding and Using Sources for Discovery

Finding and Evaluating Library and Internet Sources

1. Locate five sources on a topic: 1) an academic or professional journal article, 2) a mainstream magazine article, 3) a newspaper article, and 4) two Web sites that you would consider valid for your topic. Print/copy each article in its entirety.

2. Look closely at what organization built the site or which organization is responsible for the print source; what the main purpose of the source is (general information, article, FAQ, a field journal, scholarly, historical, monograph), and the rhetorical techniques used in the presentation of the material (layout, format, information, links).

3. In your own words, write a brief summary of each source. What are the main points?

4. For each source, write a paragraph evaluating it. Include your opinions on the source's publication date, the author's credibility or reputation, the type of source, possible bias in the source, and readability.

5. Write an MLA works cited entry for each source.

6. Attach a copy of each source.

▶ *For more information on finding and evaluating library and Internet sources, see pp. 342–58 in* Concise A&B.

Exploratory Narrative

As you work through your source material, an exploratory narrative will allow you to detail your thought process about the topic while you research it.

1. Once you've chosen your topic, find at least five sources on that topic, at least four of which must be academic articles or books.

2. At the beginning of your essay, explain why you are interested in your topic, why you think it's significant, and what answers you are finding in relation to your research question.

3. For each source, write a well-developed summary that states clearly the name of the source, its author, and other publication context. Within the same paragraph, write a response to that source that analyzes how the source shaped your thinking and how you might use it for your paper; use evidence in the form of quotations.

4. The essay should also have a conclusion that indicates where you are at the end of the process.

    Complete a full works cited page with proper MLA citation for each source.

▶ *For more information on reading strategies, see* Concise A&B *pp. 82–88. For more information on summary strategies, see* Concise A&B *pp. 88–92.*

Developing an Annotated Bibliography

An annotated bibliography will help you further explore your sources and will allow you to create a resource for others interested in your topic. Find four reputable sources you plan to use in your research essay.

1. At the top of your assignment, write a tentative thesis statement or the question guiding your research.

2. For each entry write:

    a. a properly formatted citation for the source;

    b. a paragraph that summarizes the source and details key information used to support the author's argument;

    c. a paragraph explaining how the source relates to your topic, how you plan to use the source in your paper (i.e., background information, context on the topic, an argument in support of your claim, or a counterargument), and how it extends or changes your thinking about your own project.

▶ *For more information on creating an effective annotated bibliography, see* Concise A&B *pp. 131–35. For more information on properly citing sources, see* Concise A&B *pp. 359–71.*

C. Entering the Conversation

Creating a Dialogue

Research is a social process—a conversation with people who each contribute varying ideas, facts, and theories surrounding a topic. It is important for you to understand that conversation in order to take part in it yourself. By creating a conversation among your sources and yourself, you will be better able to visualize the scope of your subject and the role each of your sources play. This process will help you discover how you might use each source in your own project and how your ideas and argument fit into the larger discussion.

1. Imagine that you are the host of a talk show themed around the topic of your research.

2. Select three or four of your sources to act as contestants on the show.

3. Try to choose sources that have different perspectives on your topic.

4. Write out three or four questions for each source. For instance, you might ask them to explain their perspective on your research topic or ask them to describe their expertise on the topic.

5. Then, using material from the source itself (quotes, information from the publisher, or details about the author), create answers to the questions from each of your sources.

6. As the moderator of the panel, you should pose questions to your sources and respond to their "responses."

Acknowledging Oppositions

At this point in your research, you should have a thorough understanding of the context around your topic and the position you wish to take. To make a well-balanced and reasoned argument, you need to consider strong and feasible oppositions to the argument you're making. Understanding and meaningfully addressing dissenting views is critical, even central, to the art of persuasion. If you ignore or minimize the views your audience may already hold, you risk losing the opportunity to change their thinking. Deeply engaging oppositions, moreover, can shape your argument by helping you see aspects of the issue you hadn't previously considered.

Find two sources that represent dissenting points of view on your issue/topic. Read them carefully.

1. Re-create the following chart. Begin by summarizing your claim or argument.

2. Using one of the sources you've found thus far, briefly describe the argument that the source is making that supports your claim.

3. In the next cell, write a question or point of disagreement an opposing viewpoint might raise, based on what you've read in your dissenting sources. (As sometimes it's difficult to think outside of your own perspective, your instructor may have you work in groups to pose questions for each other). Re-create the chart and repeat the steps using another of your sources.

4. Consider how you can answer these questions or concerns—what are some strategies you can use to help reduce the impact of these opposing points of view? Do you just need to acknowledge them, but claim your view outweighs them? Is there a flawed assumption or false concern in the opposition? Does the opposition usefully qualify or bring complexity to your own argument?

YOUR CLAIM	
Name of a source supporting your claim	
Source's argument that supports your claim	
Question(s) that the opposition would ask, or concerns they'd raise	
How can you respond?	

Once you've thought in detail about opposing viewpoints, write a reflection that considers the following questions: What do you know now about your topic that you didn't before? What are some of the flaws with both your own claims and those of your opposition? How will considering opposing views strengthen your argument? How will you address opposing views in your essay?

The Five Ws and One H
Approach your topic by posing answers to the five Ws and one H questions: Who, what, where, when, why, and how.

Cubing

Cubing allows you to come to an understanding of your topic from six different perspectives. Like approaching each side of a cube, each perspective will present a different point of view. Cubing is a timed exercise much like freewriting, except you'll spend an allotted amount of time on each side of the cube.

1. Write your topic or thesis statement at the top of a page.

2. Allot 3–5 minutes to develop each perspective of the cube: A) Describe the topic (What defines it? Use your senses as well as your mind.); B) Compare it (What is it similar to or different from?); C) Associate it (What does it make you think of? People, places, things, feelings?); D) Analyze it (What parts or components make it up? What are its traits or attributes?); E) Apply it (What can you do with it? How can you use it?); F) Argue it (What arguments are for or against it?).

Thought Letter

Write a letter or e-mail message about your topic to a friend or family member, explaining to them what interests you about it and what questions or problems it poses for you.

Metaphor or Extended Analogy

Use templates to recharge your thinking about your topic and take it in surprising directions. Try exercises such as "This topic is like _____;" or "This topic is like _____, but it is also like (or unlike);" or "If this topic were a _____, it would be like _____." Extend your metaphor or analogy into at least a page of single-spaced writing.

Examples: "Writing is like walking through tall grass." "Writing is like running, but it is also like scuba diving." "If writing were like driving a car, I'd have had a thousand crashes by now."

Conducting an Interview

The point of this activity is to interview someone who can address your questions with some expertise. Find professionals who specialize or possess noteworthy experience in your area of interest. Once you identify several possible candidates, contact them via e-mail, phone, or in person. Be sure to explain the purpose of the interview and to describe your research project clearly and succinctly. Then ask the candidate if he/she would be willing to meet with you, and, if so, what dates/times work best. You should indicate the date you wish to conduct the interview, preferably well in advance of the assignment deadline. You might also ask if you can record the interview. Keep in mind that the interview can fall through, so it is wise to have a backup plan.

▶ *For more information on conducting an interview, see the Purdue Owl Online Writing Lab Resources for conducting interviews (http://owl.english.purdue.edu/owl/resource/559/04/).*

Constructing a Questionnaire

Develop a set of questions related to your research project that will provide you with relevant information. Remember that participants will respond best to questionnaires that are clear and easy to complete.

▶ *For more information on constructing a questionnaire, see the Purdue Owl Online Writing Lab Resources for conducting surveys (http://owl.english.purdue.edu/owl/resource/559/05/).*

What Else?

Draft a list of what you still don't know about your topic. How would you find this information?

D. Determining a Focus and Mapping a Plan

Moving from Topic to Plan

In order to avoid what *Allyn & Bacon*'s editors call a "data dump," you will need to develop a claim about your topic. After doing some initial research on your topic, write a three-paragraph exploration to narrow your focus and develop a possible claim.

1. In the first paragraph, introduce your research paper topic and describe what you think the main focus of the project might be. Include a working thesis in this paragraph, which you can revise later.

2. In the second paragraph, discuss what others have said about this issue, referencing your sources specifically and anticipating additional research you may have to do.

3. In the third paragraph, speculate on what obstacles you foresee in this project and/or what you anticipate to be the most difficult part of the assignment.

Considering a Thesis

To develop a strong thesis, write what you believe your reader thinks about your topic before reading your essay and then how your reader will think differently about your topic after reading your essay. Now turn to *Concise A&B* pp. 32–37 in order to review and implement strategies by which you can change a reader's view of your topic, develop a thesis statement with tension, and surprise a reader. Draft several versions of your thesis statement with these strategies in mind and exchange with a partner for discussion and feedback.

Mapping Your Ideas

1. After you have gathered your research, taken purposeful notes, and considered the is-sue thoroughly, you may find that you are overwhelmed with information. By putting that information in a visual form, you may discover connections and patterns that can be used to structure your paper.

2. First, take ten to fifteen minutes and list everything you can about your topic. Don't worry about whether it is relevant; if you think it, write it.

3. Now, using your topic as a focal point, map out items from your list, drawing con-nections between items. You can use different colors or shapes to group and categorize items as well.

Outlining an Argument

Drawing on the material you have generated for your topic, research question, and source material, start to categorize what material will be included in which sections of the essay and sketch a possible order for those sections. It may help to have your thesis statement (or a draft of it) written out at the top of the page so that you can be sure all your points relate directly back to your thesis. Your outline may be formatted in a number of ways, but it should provide a blueprint of your argument that you can use to draft your paper.

▶ *For more information on how to create an outline and visualizing your argument, see* Concise A&B *pp. 294–98.*

E. Proposing Your Research Project

Drafting Your Research Proposal

After you have explored your topic by writing about it and conducting some preliminary research, gather your ideas in the form of a proposal that you will submit to your instruc-tor. The type of proposal you'll write for this research step differs from those described in *Concise A&B* Chapter 10, which propose solutions to problems. Instead, we're asking for one that more closely resembles those submitted in response to calls for papers written for academic journals or conferences. For this type of proposal, your readers assume that through the preliminary research you've been conducting, you have developed a position on a topic or issue that you wish to explore further, and that will, in this case, result in an extended essay.

Your proposal should include:

- A **working title**.

- The **research question** you've been exploring.

- Your **claim** or thesis supported by **reasons for your position**.

- A **discussion section** where you identify the contexts in which the question is situated: To what conversation are you adding your voice? What have others said about your topic/question? Draw on the research/reading you've done so far and think about what kind of information will be important for an outsider to know.

- A **research plan** where you outline the trajectory of your paper: How will you organize your paper? What path will it follow? What other research do you need to accomplish to finish the paper?

- A **biographical note** that explains your interest and background and expertise with regard to the topic.

▶ *For more information on developing thesis statements out of questions, see* Concise A&B *pp. 32–37.*

Presenting Your Research Proposal

This assignment requires you to create a brief presentation of your researched argument essay. Your goal is to identify for your audience the central question(s) that will guide your essay. In addition, your presentation should make clear what's at stake in your argument by offering a preliminary claim as well as a discussion of your sources. Be sure to include your plan for next steps toward completing the argument. Your instructor will determine the format (i.e., oral, visual, or both), length, and number of sources required for the presentation.

Part Two: Researched Argument

PURPOSE

A researched argument involves close reading, summary, rhetorical analysis, and synthesis and asks that you develop an extended persuasive argument using research in an appropriate and convincing way. This assignment puts particular emphasis on your ability to articulate a strong question that you refine through drafting and revision. We include a researched argument in first-year composition because thinking critically prepares you to understand and respond to debatable issues in reading, writing, and life.

FORMAT

6–8 pages or 2100–2800 words, MLA format

ASSIGNMENT DESCRIPTION

Crafting a researched argument calls on you, the writer, to identify arguable issues, take a position, and consider and respond to other perspectives that might conflict with or challenge your own. We encourage you to approach your researched argument with this view of research writing in mind; doing so, we hope, will make the writing meaningful, in addition to fulfilling the assignment.

GOALS

* Participate in and contribute to the larger conversation around your topic.

* Understand research as inquiry-based, that is, as that which evolves from informed, well-crafted questions.

* Understand that argument is rhetorically complex and not reducible to pro/con positions.

* Articulate a claim and support it with relevant, timely evidence.

* Acknowledge counter-claims while maintaining control of your argument.

* Select and balance a variety of sources that relate to your argument.

* Integrate source material by quoting, paraphrasing, and summarizing.

* Develop and sustain an idea through a well-organized, thesis-driven essay supported with relevant evidence and examples.

* Demonstrate reasonable sentence-level control, including syntax and grammar competency, and cite source material using MLA conventions.

A&B REFERENCES: CONDUCTING RESEARCH

Writing as a Problem-Solving Process, pp. 276–289

Evaluating Sources for Reliability, Credibility, Angle of Vision, and Degree of Advocacy, pp. 342–345

Know When and How to Use Summary, Paraphrase, and Quotation, pp. 348–350

Use Attributive Tags, pp. 351–355

Avoid Plagiarism, pp. 355–356

Citing and Documenting Sources, pp. 359–366

CONSTRUCTING AN ARGUMENT

Exploring Problems, Making Claims, pp. 22–40

Writing a Classical Argument, pp. 202–228

Strategies for Writing Closed-Form Prose, pp. 290–317

How Messages Persuade, pp. 42–56

ACTIVITIES: COMPOSE REVISE REFLECT

a. Imagine appearing on a talk show to present your research. How would you describe your research and argument to a general, T.V. audience? What evidence is most compelling? Where do you think you are addressing your opposition most strongly? What are you adding to the conversation about your topic? Use this informal script as a guide for revising before you submit your final draft.

b. Think back to the beginning of the semester and the skills you used in your Texts in Action essay. Review that section of the *Student Guide* and any notes you have about reading rhetorically. After you have done this, analyze your essay in terms of the rhetorical devices you have used in this draft of your paper. Take notes on each paragraph to see how you use the art of persuasion in your work. How is your language used to change the attitudes or beliefs of your audience? What expert evidence have you incorporated to persuade your opposition? How do you use logic? What is the tone of your essay? How have you addressed the opposition in a respectful way? After you take notes, revise your essay in places where you could be more rhetorically effective.

c. Examine your introduction and your conclusion. These are significant places in your essay where you build a bridge to your audience and where you conclude your argument. Choose an essay or other piece of writing you've read during the term and explore how that writer crafts their introduction and conclusion. Is there a technique that you could use in your essay? Is there a story that you have read about in your research that you could begin with that illustrates your thesis? Is there a personal experience you have had in your life that you could begin with to build your ethos? If so, revise these important parts of your essay.

d. In the University of Cincinnati's first graduating class of 1878, all eight students were required to write a baccalaureate essay intended to "grapple with social problems" and to read their essay at their graduation ceremony at Pike's Opera House. All these many years later, you have now entered into an academic tradition by writing the Researched Argument genre. Now look at the final mini-workshop called Genre. How does your essay fulfill the genre expectations? Is there anywhere where you break the genre? Is this break purposeful? Write a short paragraph reflecting on how your work fits into this long tradition.

e. Descriptive Verbs and Attributive Tags

    When introducing quotations and/or paraphrased ideas in an attributive tag, it can be tempting to repeat the standard "says" or "states" for every source. But carefully considered verbs can have great effect; not only will your sentences have more energy and variety, but you can also affect your readers' perspective on the incorporated source material.

adds
speculates
concludes
sees
explains
asks
refuses
contends
illustrates
claims
reports
denies
warns
maintains
concedes
emphasizes
argues
points out
considers
notes
holds
believes
relates
defends
thinks
insists
compares
suggests
disputes
agrees
observes
condemns
shows
finds
rejects
declares
reveals
implies
comments
responds
disagrees
writes

1. Read through a draft of your researched argument essay and locate a quote or paraphrase introduced with a simple "says" or "states." Choose a more fitting descriptive verb from the list provided, or choose your own. Write the revised sentence here:

2. How does this small verb change help your reader see or understand the source material differently? What other information might the reader benefit from knowing about this source material?

3. Next, inspect each quote or paraphrase in your draft. Write or revise the attributive tags with descriptive verbs for each (see *Concise A&B* pp. 351–353 for more details on attributive tags). Be sure that any quoted sentence isn't standing alone (this is called a dropped quote). Also, be sure that after each quote/paraphrase, you have explained how it relates to and supports your argument as this is an important connection to make clear to your reader. The following is an easy "formula" to keep in mind:

Intro source with an attributive tag and descriptive verb

+

"Quotation" or paraphrase (citation)

+

How the quote/paraphrase relates to your point

=

A well-incorporated source

UNIT 3

RECASTING FOR A PUBLIC AUDIENCE

Photo from the Clothesline Project on McMicken Commons, April 2016. Credit Joyce Malek.
Copyright 2017 by Department of English, University of Cincinnati. All rights reserved.

PURPOSE

This assignment asks that you reconsider the purpose, goals, and focus of your researched argument essay. This assignment builds on what you learned about rhetorical concepts like genre, audience, and context from the mini-workshops and earlier essays. Because you need to repurpose your researched argument in a new medium and for a different audience, you will have an opportunity to refocus your research and consider the challenges that come with presenting your message in a new form. This assignment prepares you to do the kinds of thinking and writing required to successfully communicate a message to various discourse communities, whether the community is formal or informal, familiar or unfamiliar, academic or nonacademic. This assignment also asks you to work with genre, one of the areas emphasized in Intermediate Composition, the second course in the English Composition sequence.

FORMAT

Determined by the option chosen and your instructor's requirements.

ASSIGNMENT DESCRIPTION

A recast involves taking an object and remodeling or reconstructing it. For this assignment, you'll take the focus of your research argument essay and "recast" it into a new medium, with a different audience and focus in mind. The goals of this project are to share your work with more people than your instructor and to be aware of the various decisions that you need to make when working with different audiences and different media.

A&B *REFERENCES: RECAST*

Writer's Decisions Are Shaped by Purpose, Audience, and Genre, pp. 7–12

The Rules for "Good Writing" Vary Depending on Rhetorical Context, pp. 14–20

How Messages Persuade, pp. 42–63

Multimodal and Online Communication, pp. 66–78

Strategies for Composing Multimodal Texts, pp. 323–336

Along with your recast, you'll also write a two- to three-page rationale where you have the opportunity to reflect on the choices that went into your recast and discuss the ways your argument has grown or changed in light of those choices. In the rationale, you'll discuss your project's purpose, the form (medium or genre) of your project, the audience your recast project is directed toward, and the rhetorical choices you made in creating your recast. ***In effect, your rationale should make an argument about your project's purpose and effectiveness.***

Goals

* Understand that researched writing can be reworked for different audiences.

* Explore different genres as possibilities for your writing.

* Consider how the needs of a public audience affect choices in communicating your message.

* Demonstrate how to represent yourself through your work to a public audience.

* Demonstrate how to present your purpose and argument to best suit your audience's needs and expectations.

Options

1. Multimedia Text for *Queen City Writers*

   Recast your argument into a format acceptable for publication in the University of Cincinnati's undergraduate journal, *Queen City Writers* (http://qc-writers.com). *Queen City Writers* seeks pieces informed by research that are "related to writing, rhetoric, reading, literacy broadly conceived, popular culture and media, community discourses, and multimodal and digital composing" ("Submissions"). For the Multimedia section, present your argument using video, audio, or mixed media.

   The Multimedia section calls for an "artist's statement" that explains your "purpose, motivations, reasons for using a particular medium (what are its affordances?), intended effect, timeliness of project, and goals for use by viewers/readers." Complete this "artist's statement" in place of the recast rationale.

2. Advocacy Text

   Create an advocacy ad, public service poster, Web site, or pamphlet that recasts the issue argued in your research essay as a public problem that calls for action and support. This project calls on you to capture your argument in a highly condensed form, while making it visually clear and memorable. You will need to consider all the features of visual arguments—type sizes and fonts, layout, color, and images and graphics—to grab the attention of your audience, construct a compelling sketch of the problem, and inform your audience what course of action you want them to take.

Accompany your project with a 2-to-3-page rationale that describes and explains the choices you made in designing it. Your rationale should discuss your audience, the goal or purpose of your project, the conventions of the genre and how you met them, and the rhetorical choices you made in its composition.

3. Multimodal Text

    Recast your researched argument essay choosing one of the multimodal options described below. For more information on multimodal and online communication, refer to *Concise A&B* pp. 66–79; to learn more about strategies for composing multimodal texts in several genres, see *Concise A&B* pp. 323–339.

    a. **Video:** Recast your research argument essay as a video of approximately 3–5 minutes. Your video should capture your argument in a highly condensed form, while making the video engaging, easy to follow, and interesting to your viewers. You will need to consider how the contents of your video grab the attention of your audience, construct a compelling sketch of the problem, and inform your audience what course of action you want them to take.

    b. **Podcast:** Recast your research argument essay as a podcast of approximately 3–5 minutes. As you deliver the podcast, consider how the act of delivery changes when using a medium without visual aids. Consider structuring the podcast as an interview with your sources, adding music or other voices to make it more engaging. You will need to consider how the contents of your podcast *grab the attention* of your audience, *construct a compelling sketch of the problem*, and *inform your audience what course of action* you want them to take.

    c. **Speech Presentation with Visual Aids:** Recast your research argument essay as a prepared speech of approximately 5 minutes supported with visual aids. Your speech should *grab the attention* of your audience, *construct a compelling sketch of the problem*, and *inform your audience what course of action* you want them to take. As you deliver your speech, use appropriate visual aids to give presence to the problem, highlight points, provide memorable data or evidence, or otherwise enhance appeals to logos, ethos, and pathos.

    d. **Web Site or Blog:** Create a Web site or blog that recasts the issue argued in your research essay as a public problem and calls for action and support. This project calls on you to capture your argument in a highly condensed form, while making the site visually pleasing and easy to read and navigate. You will need to consider all the features of visual arguments—type sizes and fonts, layout, color, and images and graphics—to grab the attention of your audience, construct a compelling sketch of the problem, and inform your audience what course of action you want them to take.

e. **Zine:** Create a zine that recasts the issue argued in your research essay as a public problem and calls for action and support. According to ArtMattersBlog, a zine is "usually a non-commercial, non professional publication, kind of like a magazine but [instead of making a profit], zines add other, often unheard voices into the mix, [and that] typically zines are made using collage techniques and are then photocopied, since these are means available to almost everyone." You will need to *consider all the features of visual arguments*—type sizes and fonts, layout, color, and images and graphics—to *grab the attention* of your audience, *construct a compelling sketch of the problem*, and *inform your audience what course of action* you want them to take.

f. **Comic Strip**: Create a comic strip that recasts the issue argued in your research essay as a public problem and calls for action and support. This project calls on you to capture your argument in a highly condensed form, while making it visually clear and memorable. You will need to consider all the features of visual arguments—type sizes and fonts, layout, color, and images and graphics—to grab the attention of your audience, construct a compelling sketch of the problem, and inform your audience what course of action you want them to take.

Other options as determined by your instructor.

Student Technology Resources Center

In addition to hosting computer labs and textual resources, University of Cincinnati's Langsam Library has the Student Technology Resources Center. Check out the center's resources—such as video cameras and editing software—as you compose your recast.

Location: Fourth Floor, Langsam Library

Phone: (513) 556-1468

Web address: https://www.libraries.uc.edu/services/student-technology-resources-center.html

ACTIVITIES: COMPOSE REVISE REFLECT

a. Write a proposal for your recast. Write out the thesis statement from your research argument essay and include the following in a 1–2 page proposal designed to help you plan for the recast assignment:

- Brief description of your recast, including what purposes you are trying to achieve, the audience your recast is attempting to reach, and reasons for targeting that audience.

- Outline reasons for your choice of medium and explain why that medium is the most appropriate for your audience.

- Write about the tools and/or technology you will need to create your recast. Explain what you know about them, and how will you use them to recast your argument.

- Explain your plan for completing the recast as well as any concerns you have at this point.

b. Contact faculty in your major or career path and ask them about tools and media they use to present information to public audiences. You might find that faculty and workplaces have standards for posters, visual aids, technology and more. If you do not have a major or career path declared, you might ask a student group or consult a faculty from a course you are taking.

c. Create a Fair Use argument that helps you justify your use of multimedia in the recast. To learn more about Fair Use guidelines and how they apply to your work, visit Purdue Owl's "Strategies for Fair Use" (https://owl.english.purdue.edu/owl/resource/731/1/). Write a paragraph describing how your recast meets the four Fair Use guidelines. For more information on copyright, Fair Use, and creative commons licenses, see *Concise A&B* pp. 74–77.

d. Imagine an ideal reader or audience for your recast project. What interests your reader? What is your reader most passionate about? What activities, groups, or organizations is your reader involved in? What would your reader find most intriguing about your project? What do you expect that your reader will do or think after reading or viewing your project? What would your reader want to talk to you about after reading or viewing your project? What would you like to tell your reader about your project?

e. Reflect on yourself as a researcher. Now that you've composed your research argument essay, think about how you come across to your readers. How is your expertise highlighted? How did you build credibility in your research essay (think about the sources you used, how you connected to your reader, and your writing style)? How will you reproduce that ethos in your recast assignment?

UNIT 4

REFLECTING ON YOUR WORK

Photo from the *UC Drawn* exhibit from UC's Philip M. Meyers, Jr. Memorial Gallery, 2015. Credit Chris Carter and Joyce Malek. Copyright 2017 by Department of English, University of Cincinnati. All rights reserved.

KEY ASSIGNMENT

Write a reflective essay, letter, or narrative of your writing experiences that grows out of the writing and revising you did this semester, with particular emphasis on how you hope to transfer what you learned in this class to other writing situations.

PURPOSE

This unit reinforces and formalizes reflection as a skill central to effective writing practice. Getting in the habit of thinking critically about your writing will help you develop strong revising skills and become a self-directed writer capable of reentering an essay to improve it. The practice of reflection—becoming aware of your writing processes, and examining the characteristics of your writing, including its strengths and weaknesses—nurtures habits that will serve you well in any writing situation.

FORMAT

* 3–4 pages

Goals

* Generate a learning narrative about your writing that candidly addresses successes, setbacks, realizations, and strategies for applying what you've learned to other situations.

* Illustrate your understanding of writing as a series of deliberate rhetorical choices that have effects.

* Apply your skills in rhetorical analysis to your own writing.

ASSIGNMENT DESCRIPTION

During the course of the semester as you have been drafting, researching, and revising, you have also been writing short, reflective pieces (i.e., in-class freewriting, process writes, directed reflections, reflecting and revising activities) about your rhetorical choices and about your experience with argument-based writing. These brief reflections allowed you to pause and consider your work as it was occurring so that you could become more aware of your learning and composing processes.

This final reflective assignment asks you to examine more comprehensively the work you have done this term by writing about the rhetorical choices you made across your writing, the processes you used to develop as a writer, and/or the habits you've learned that you can apply in future courses. Just like the analytical and argument-based writing you've been practicing all term, reflective writing requires that you select and explain specific examples from your writing that can exemplify your learning in this course.

Options

1. Analyze the rhetorical choices you made in composing the two major assignments: the researched argument essay and the recast. What parts of these works best illustrate your choices? What have you learned about the demands of audience, purpose, and genre in the process of recasting your researched argument for a public audience? How might you apply this knowledge in the future?

2. Writing and revision are ongoing, potentially endless, processes; even "final" drafts can be honed, rethought, extended, or otherwise improved. Write an evaluation of the work you're submitting as "final drafts": What are the strengths and weaknesses? What would you do to the drafts if you had more time?

ACTIVITIES: COMPOSE REVISE REFLECT

a. Look back on the writing that will appear in your portfolio and reconstruct the details of the writing processes involved in creating each one. If it helps, draw yourself working on each project. Once you've completed each reenactment, identify any useful patterns or good habits across your composing processes. Share your findings with a classmate. Then write a paragraph that describes your best writing process habits.

b. Find one sentence or moment in your writing that you like. Write a short paragraph about it that describes why and how it's effective.

c. Draw a map or a storyboard that tracks your experiences in ENGL 1001. Where did you start as a writer on the first day? At what points did you face challenges or triumphs? How are you changed as a writer at the end of the course?

d. After you've completed a draft of your reflection, read it aloud. Ask yourself if your reader can picture specific events or details about your experiences in ENGL 1001, or if you have directed them to certain moments in your writing. Can your readers *see* you and your experiences? If not, revise to include more details or specific anecdotes as evidence.

MINI-WORKSHOPS

Used courtesy of the Archives & Rare Books Library, University of Cincinnati. All rights reserved.

"Writing is not just self-expression; it is communication with the goal of affecting readers in real ways."

—Michael Berndt and Amy Muse

PURPOSE

The mini-workshops are designed as stand-alone exercises to deepen your understanding about how writing and reading work. We hope you will enjoy these activities as you make your way through the course and that you will return to them throughout your time at UC.

Writing Inventory

To help you get more out of your English Composition 1001 course and see the progress you're making over the semester, we've put together a list of skills relevant to the course. Completing the inventory will help you notice what you're learning and help your instructor to help you. This inventory is not a test of your writing proficiency or knowledge.

So that you can track your progress, fill out the inventory three times during the term, at the beginning, midway through the term, and at the end. Use a scale of 1 to 4 for each statement: 1 for no; 2 for not very well or not very easily; 3 for fairly well or fairly easily, and 4 for yes. If you don't know the answer, use a question mark. Move from left to right by filling in the lefthand column at the beginning of the term, the middle column in the middle of the term, and the righthand column at the end of the term.

Your instructor will decide whether to collect the inventory and how to use it.

My Attitude Toward Writing

—— —— ——   I enjoy writing.

—— —— ——   I think of myself as a writer.

—— —— ——   In general, I find that writing is easy for me.

—— —— ——   In general, I enjoy writing papers for my classes.

Generating Writing

—— —— ——   I can get ideas down on paper or screen fairly quickly and easily.

—— —— ——   I have several strategies to help me get my ideas on paper or screen.

—— —— ——   As I write, I am easily able to come up with ideas and insights that I didn't have before.

—— —— ——   When I'm interested in a topic, I can generate writing fairly easily and quickly and not get stuck.

—— —— ——   When I'm **not** interested in a topic, I can generate writing fairly easily and not get stuck.

Organizing My Writing

—— —— ——   Once I've generated ideas and written them down, I am able to organize my writing into a logical pattern of sentences and paragraphs.

—— —— ——   I am able to use a variety of transitional strategies to move from one idea to another within and between paragraphs.

—— —— ——   I find that writing introductions for my papers is easy for me.

—— —— ——   I am able to successfully conclude my essays.

Using Sources

___   ___   ___   I can easily find sources relevant to any topic I'm writing about.

___   ___   ___   I can cite sources correctly within my papers using an appropriate documentation format (for example, MLA, APA).

___   ___   ___   I can document sources correctly on a reference page at the end of my papers using an appropriate format (for example, MLA, APA).

___   ___   ___   I am able to summarize, paraphrase, and quote sources correctly within my paper.

___   ___   ___   I am able to frame sources effectively within my papers.

Revising My Writing

___   ___   ___   I am able to step back from my writing and "re-see" it to make substantive changes.

___   ___   ___   I view revising as a way to generate ideas and to clarify them.

___   ___   ___   I am able to revise my writing so that my purpose is clear to my readers.

___   ___   ___   I am able to revise my writing to better fit readers' needs and expectations.

___   ___   ___   I am able to revise my writing to make my sentences livelier.

Editing My Writing

___   ___   ___   I view editing as an important part of my writing process.

___   ___   ___   I am able to correct mistakes in grammar, spelling, punctuation, and other mechanical errors when I edit.

Getting and Giving Feedback on Writing

___ ___ ___ I enjoy sharing my writing with others for their responses and feedback.

___ ___ ___ I am able to read aloud my work to others without apologies or holding back.

___ ___ ___ I am able to listen openly to feedback and reactions to my writing.

___ ___ ___ I am able to make changes to my writing based on feedback from others.

___ ___ ___ I am able to respond to specific passages by telling my peers how the writing is affecting me or by telling them what I hear the words saying.

___ ___ ___ I am able to comment on my peers' ideas, raise questions, and offer specific revision recommendations.

Reflecting on My Writing

___ ___ ___ I am able to give an account of my writing process, the steps in my process.

___ ___ ___ I am able to give an account of the thoughts and feelings I have as I am writing.

___ ___ ___ I am able to analyze my writing process, notice areas that are causing me problems, and take steps to resolve them.

___ ___ ___ I am able to apply what I learn from analyzing my writing to writing that I do in other classes, or for other readers and purposes.

Adapted from pages 447–449 of *A Community of Writers: A Workshop Course in Writing*, 3rd edition by Peter Elbow and Pat Belanoff. Copyright © 1999 McGraw-Hill Education. Used with permission.

How I Write

Discussion

Writing is more than assignments completed for classes. From posting to Facebook, to texting and tweeting, to creating blogs and websites, across platforms and places, we're writing more than ever. This mini-workshop asks you to consider your writing processes and practices, your thoughts and feelings about writing, and how, where, and why you write, with what, and for whom.

Options

1. Keep a writing log. Pick a period of time, say one day or one week, and keep track of all of the writing that you do. Divide your log into columns or sections labeled "What I'm writing," "Why I'm writing," "Who I'm writing to/for," "When and Where I'm writing," and "With what I'm writing." At the end of the time period, tally up your responses. Then write a reflection about what you discovered about your everyday writing practices.

2. Focusing on writing you did for a project or assignment, write about a time when writing went particularly well. Try to capture in as much detail as you can what made it go well. For example, where did you write? When did you write? What tools did you use (computer, paper, pen, etc.)? What was happening around you as you wrote? What feelings and thoughts did you have as you wrote? Did you talk about or share your writing with others?

3. Conversely, write about a time when writing didn't go so well. What got in the way of your being able to write? What did you do to complete the writing task?

4. Trace your writing process as you write a paper for a class. Over the next several weeks as you write and revise papers for this class, keep a log of the steps you take in writing and the amount of time you spend generating or brainstorming ideas, reading, drafting, revising, editing, sharing your work with others, and so on. Note, too, the thoughts and feelings you have as you write. Write a reflection about what you notice and learn about your writing process.

5. Look up an interview with a well-known or favorite writer online at *The Paris Review* http://www.theparisreview.org/interviews and read what they say about their writing practices. What did you learn? What surprised you? How do their processes or concerns compare with yours?

Goals

* To notice how much writing you do everyday and how much you transfer knowledge about writing across writing tasks and activities

* To recognize your agency in your writing practices and processes and see that you can control the circumstances under which you write

- To notice how writing is affected by rhetorical choices guided by purpose, audience, genre, and situation.

How I Read

Discussion

Reading is a complex rhetorical process that we often take for granted. This mini-workshop asks you to think about your process of reading and how those processes are influenced by decisions writers make to fulfill an intended purpose.

Options

1. Explain your reading experience in relation to a text. What were your first impressions? Which of the author's words, ideas, format choices, structure, or other features were responsible for those impressions? As you continued to read, how did your impressions change, build, or get confirmed? Describe the author's rhetorical moves: methods of establishing his/her credibility, order or arrangement of material, use of source material, stylistic patterns, or efforts to reach out a particular audience. If you think of the text as a designed space in which everything exists for a reason, where did you most question why the writer was making certain choices? At which points in the text were you most connected to the reading? At which points were you least connected? Explore why you think this is so. Given your responses, what sort of conclusions can you draw about the text, the writer, and yourself as a reader?

2. Take a "reading selfie." Take a picture of a space in which you are reading. Write a caption that describes the scene of your reading, including what, where, and when you're reading. Using this image, your "reading selfie," as a point of departure, write a reflection about how the environment affected your reading processes. For example, make note of the noise level, people, furniture, nearby objects, technologies, and activities you are doing while reading. You might also record distractions and describe any rituals you have for the kind of reading you're doing. Finally, note the strategies you use when reading, like taking notes, underlining, or writing comments in the margins. Based on what you noticed, write about how the material, spatial, and temporal environment enabled and supported your reading process. Would another reading environment be preferable? Why or why not? What did writing about how you read help you see about yourself as a reader?

    Optional: Post your reading selfie and caption to a shared blog or Web site, or share them with your classmates on social media using a class hashtag (#).

3. Read aloud a piece of writing as if you were performing it for an audience, paying particular attention to how the text affects your delivery. You might choose to read a piece of writing with unusual punctuation or one that uses especially descriptive language: a poem or brief prose passage would work well, but you might want to experiment with

a text that isn't traditionally read aloud, such as a syllabus or a test. What gestures or facial expressions did you use and what body position or stance did you take? How did you "perform" a dash or parentheses? A list? How did you portray the emotion or feeling behind a strong image or series of descriptive phrases? Write about the choices you made in your performance, and what insights it provided about the text and your reading process.

4. Document and analyze another person's reading process. With permission, make detailed observations of another person reading. Take notes as your subject reads, paying attention to how the reader is positioned, where focus seems to wander, and where the reader seems most engaged, confused, or inattentive. Does the reader take notes or annotate the text? Interview your subject about her typical reading process and about what you observed. Write about your observations and interview. What did you learn? What surprised you? Discuss what this activity suggests about how we read.

Goals

- Understand and appreciate the relationship between reader and writer.

- View reading as a mental *and* physical activity.

- See reading and writing as processes that require self-awareness, practice, and skill.

- Recognize that different types of texts make demands on readers that shift based on style, genre, situation, and purpose.

- Apply the concept of rhetorical situation to analysis of writing and reading practices.

Voice

Discussion

When we talk about a writer's "voice," we talk about how the writing sounds. But what makes writing sound one way or another? In fact, the sound of a piece of writing, its voice, is often about sentence-level stuff, like length of sentences, the use or absence of coordinating elements, punctuation, word choice, conventional or deviant forms of spelling, and so on. When we write, the voice we use is determined by our readers or audience, our purpose, and the role or relationship we hope to establish with our audience. These activities in persuasion help us notice how differences in audience, purpose, and writer/reader roles affect how we write.

▶   *For more on voice, see* Concise A&B *pp. 55–56.*

Options

1. Choose one card from two stacks your instructor will give you: One card will state a topic and the second will state an audience. Your goal is to write about your topic in a way that will persuade your audience to care about it or appreciate its importance. Take notes about how you adapted your writing "voice" to achieve this aim. What aspects of your topic did you emphasize and how did you draw attention to those aspects through choice of sentence length, level of diction, punctuation, repetition, word choice, and so forth? Include a one-paragraph reflection of the choices you made: what did you notice about the relationship between audience and voice?

2. Select a short written passage, performance, or other type of text and *recast* it in a different medium. You might rewrite a text that was originally serious (like a political speech) as a stand-up comedy act, or conversely, transform a humorous piece (like a stand-up comedy act) into a political speech. In a short response, describe what you did to recast the material for a different purpose.

3. Choose an artist (writer, speaker, singer, choreographer, etc.) whose "voice" you find particularly compelling. Write about the features of this person's creative expression that make you return to her/his work. Be as specific as possible, noting patterns across two or more pieces of the artist's work.

4. Record yourself reading aloud from either your own written work or from a favorite piece authored by someone else. When you listen to your reading, what do you notice? Does your voice increase your appreciation or understanding of the work? Did the act of reading aloud produce any surprises? What elements of the text are more or less compelling when you hear it aloud? When you write about the experience, reflect on how what you learned might translate to your writing.

Goals

*   Demonstrate how purpose and audience affect the choices we make in connecting voice and persuasion.

*   Understand that reading and writing are rhetorical activities that produce specific effects on audiences.

*   Experience writing as a powerful medium for action.

Style

Discussion

What we say and how we say it are interconnected. The activities below foster a view of language as playful and fluid, rather than strictly rule-governed.

▶ *For more on style, see* Concise A&B *pp. 50–52.*

Options

1. Choose a passage of writing, either fiction or nonfiction. Then highlight or underline every verb or verb phrase in the passage. Based on what you notice about the verbs, create a character sketch of the writer or character. Write about how you arrived at this description, making a special point to indicate how the verbs influence the effect of the passage.

2. Divide a piece of paper (or screen) into three columns. Mark the first column "what's being said," the second, "how it's being said," and the third, "commentary and invention." In the **first column**, record a passage (approximately a paragraph) of your own writing; beneath it, explain what you wanted to express in the passage, elaborating on and providing more context about the original. In the **second column**, comment on how you wrote the passage, focusing on your use of tone, style, voice, specific words, and sentence structures. In the **third column**, create a revision of at least one sentence from this passage and explain your goal for revising. Goals could include anything from a desire to better coordinate your thought and expression, to experimentation that allows you to try out a different approach.

3. Choose a passage of several sentences (or one long sentence) from a favorite writer and imitate its form. Copy the passage or sentence out in longhand so that you get a felt sense of how the writing is crafted. Be sure to copy it exactly as it's written, paying attention to punctuation, use of capital letters, breaks, spacing, and so on. Then using the same structure, substitute your own words in an imitation. Jot a few notes about what you noticed when you copied the original passage or sentence and when you imitated it.

4. Select a sentence from a draft of your writing. Rewrite that sentence using a different structure, word order, etc., but maintain the original meaning. Continue to rewrite that sentence five or ten different ways. Once you've crafted all these variations, write a short response that reflects on the process of creating these variations and also which variation you find most effective and why.

5. Keep a "commonplace" notebook of brief passages, quotes, sayings, or other small texts that convey interesting turns of language or ways of writing. Focusing on the *how* of the writing instead of the *what*, follow each example with your analysis of what makes the writing stylistically interesting to you.

Goals

*   Experience the ways in which *how* something is written affects what we perceive about writers, characters, messages, and intent.

*   Analyze what writers do to construct a persona and deliver a message.

*   Develop an "ear" for reading and hearing different styles writers use.

*   Experiment with changing language and style to produce different effects.

Context

Discussion

All writing happens within a context. This mini-workshop asks you to consider how context influences written, visual, and spoken text.

Options

1. Context, broadly defined, is the set of circumstances surrounding an object of analysis. Research the context of a written, visual, or spoken piece of language and consider how context affects other rhetorical elements. Aspects of context may include:

- Date of writing, production, publication, or presentation.

- Publication or dissemination type, genre.

- Availability of the text.

- Issues of the text's historical moment.

- Ongoing debates related to the text's content.

- Cultural concerns, events, or creative works with which the text was in conversation.

Goals
- Recognize that texts react to various debates or conversations, become part of the conversation, and change over time.

- Notice the effects that context has on the style, rhetorical choices, or genre of discourse.

Genre

Discussion

Genres are the forms discourse takes to accomplish certain goals. By understanding the conventions and rhetorical purposes of particular genres, writers are better able to meet the expectations of readers, and readers are better able to understand and respond appropriately.

Options

1. Collect several pieces of writing of the same genre; for example, three or four syllabi, lab reports, recipes, product instructions, blog postings, acknowledgements, and so on. Ignoring what the texts *say*, describe them as if they were objects by focusing on their appearance or components. For example, notice the line breaks, lengths of paragraphs and sentences, spacing, use of italics, boldface, bullet points, and so on. After describing how the texts look, write about what the appearance of the pieces reveals about the expectations or conventions of the genre.

2. Recast a genre in the form of another genre. For example, rewrite a horoscope or obituary in the form of a poem or a poem in the form of a recipe. Then write about what you did to recast the genre. How did the recast change your reading of the genre? How did this task require different thinking about language, purpose, and audience?

3. Find two pieces of writing on the same subject written for two different purposes or audiences. Describe how the format, use of images, vocabulary, syntax, and so on, differ between the two texts and how the genre responds to reader's needs and expectations.

Goals

- Understand that genre conventions develop for specific rhetorical purposes.
- Articulate how genres inform the way we compose and influence the way we read.
- Analyze how purpose and audience shape and are shaped by the choice of genre.

WELCOME TO THE GUIDE
UNITS
MINI-WORKSHOPS
STUDENT WRITING

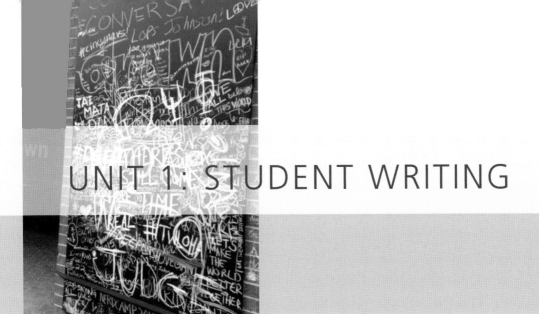

UNIT 1: STUDENT WRITING

Copyright 2017 by Department of English, University of Cincinnati. All rights reserved.

Texts in Action

Analysis of the structure, purpose, and effects of a text is a skill with broad application. In this section, we feature four interpretations of the Texts in Action assignment, including Alison Arnone's examination of an opinion editorial on technological literacy, Zac Davis's analysis of a TED Talk, and Connor Howard's study of a "Got Milk?" advertisement. We hope that these examples demonstrate some of the ways that we can unpack and interpret the features of written and visual texts.

Your instructor may ask you to produce a different genre or structure for this assignment, but every Texts in Action essay should work to explain how a text acts to influence beliefs, behaviors, and attitudes in an audience.

The featured essays describe how language is used, how the text is put together, and what effects the text seeks to have on its intended audience(s).

Some questions to stimulate discussion of the samples or your own drafts:

- How does the writer demonstrate and discuss the purpose of the text?

- Does the writer make an argument? Is the argument authoritative? Why? In what ways is the writer persuasive?

- How does the writer use specific examples to unpack how the features of the text are used?

- What is the structure of the essay? How does the writer move from one concept or idea to the next? How well does the structure work to explain the subject text?

Alison Arnone

Professor Nordgren

English 1001

21 September 2015

From Twitter to Tone: A Rhetorical Analysis

How many times does an average person check their phone a day? Believe it or not, there have been real studies to find out the answer to this question, and according to one, it's about 110 times a day (Woollaston). 110 times "sliding to unlock" may seem like a fairly large number, but of all the information and entertainment that's available through the technology that fits in the palm of a person's hand, 110 may not seem like enough. The world has come a long way, and with new inventions being revealed every day, it's hard to keep up and restrain from being distracted by the new gadgets. Technology has become woven into every part of life and in some cases, the elimination or even a reduction of technology could result in horrible consequences. In the article "Mind Over Mass Media," the myths of technology taking over our lives is debunked by Steven Pinker. Using several different rhetorical techniques like tone and audience awareness, Pinker makes his argument that mass media is not corrupting brains like society is trying to portray.

2

Steven Pinker, a professor at Harvard University, is a writer for the *New York Times* and is most famous for his research on vision, language, and social relations and for the books and other publications he authored that correspond with those topics ("About"). By studying and understanding the mind and language, he wrote the very interesting article "Mind Over Mass Media" on a subject with a twist that used previous work and knowledge. As the rhetor, his goal and purpose is to inform and convince his audience that mass and social media are not corrupting life as much as what society is telling the world, and if we take the right steps and set limits, self-control is possible.

This article is considered an opinion editorial which means that Pinker is trying to sway his audience towards his opinion. At the end of the article, he states his name and profession but never uses any pronouns in the article. Although he doesn't give his credentials directly, readers can assume that Pinker has gone through the same things as they have when it comes to the constant checking of some form of technology. The *New York Times* in the hard-copy form tends to have a target audience that is older, but as times change and technology improves, the target audience of the paper, and this article, has a lower age average. Access to the Internet on smartphones, tablets, and computers make this article available to anyone

3

which opens the target audience age to a large zone but still keeps the average in the younger bracket.

An example of how Pinker manages to appeal to the younger audience is in the paragraph where he mentions that "[habits of deep reflection] must be acquired in special institutions which we call universities" (Pinker). By mentioning universities and the importance of them, the younger generation is able to connect with his argument because they are less removed from their college experiences. The topic of the paper also points toward more of a younger audience. As people get older, their lack of interest in social media and technology may decline because they may not understand the purpose of the small computers that we keep in our pockets and check religiously, but if they were to continue reading past the title, they would find out that the article has examples that they could relate to.

Word choice will also affect the audience; the higher levels of vocabulary will attract an older, more educated audience and the *New York Times* tends to have the association of an educated audience, but that does not mean that the younger generations of adults that this article was written for won't understand. Overall, Pinker's diction in the article is appropriate which creates a well-balanced age range of younger and older readers and also contributes to his appeal of ethics; still, his topic and argument skew the range of age to an older demographic.

4

On page four, Pinker uses two sources, Woody Allen's interpretation of "War and Peace" and "The Invisible Gorilla: and Other Ways Our Intuitions Deceive Us," to support his claims (Pinker). By including these sources, it establishes Pinker's ethos since it shows his audience that he has found other sources that support his own claims. Also, by stating specific social media platforms and electronics like Twitter and Blackberry, he is convincing his audience that he has authority on the subject.

Another appeal Pinker uses is logos, or the appeal to logic, by persuading his audience that mass media and the new and improving technology is not as deadly as it may seem. One example of this use of logos is on page one, where Pinker states that "If electronic media were hazardous to intelligence, the quality of science would be plummeting. Yet discoveries are multiplying like fruit flies." By stating this piece of information as an "if...then," Pinker is easily able to counter with a logical argument that makes sense to everyone who reads the article. Pinker is effective in making logical statements that are easy to understand and keep the tone of the article the same.

As Pinker introduces a claim and counters it with a better argument, the intended tone of the paper seems to establish itself. The overall tone seems derogatory but hopeful, and is evident when he mentions a critic or claim and shoots it

5

down with no mercy but then follows up with a suggestion or an argument that disproves the claim. Although he does not directly state that the original claim is wrong, he provides examples and evidence to give the audience hope in their technology and lifestyle. An example of this strategy is on page three when Pinker states that the constant arrival of information is distracting and addictive, but follows up with a suggestion to turn off the electronics or social media sites for a small period of time to set self-control. Even the title, "Mind Over Mass Media," implies that we have a choice to make and although it may not be the easiest, it has the potential to change our lives for the better. Pinker's tone also indicates that he has obviously fallen victim to new technologies, but he knows that they're important to our society and culture. If new technology wasn't performing the way it should have, it would not have survived.

Every type of literature, whether it is a book, an article, or even a poem, has a purpose, and its effectiveness depends on how well the piece achieves the purpose. Since Pinker's goal and purpose was to get the audience to think of his beliefs and agree with them, he had to explain why his opinion was worth believing in. By putting quick, direct sentences like "Far from making us stupid, these technologies are the only things that are keeping us smart" into his article, Pinker forces his audience to think about that one sentence, and even if it was only for a second,

6

the goal was achieved. A direct sentence like that is a very effective way to sway the audience to a side because it will stimulate their thought process and create a micro-debate within their own head. Slowly but surely the belief the reader originally had is turned into more of the rhetor's beliefs. By using certain words and creating sentences that make the audience think about the piece, Pinker achieves his goal of swaying the views of the readers, making his article very effective.

As Pinker points out in the first sentence of the article, "New forms of media have always caused moral panic." Time will increase and technology will improve, but that quote will always stay true because of society's fear of moving on. Pinker has his audience hooked from this sentence and throughout his article using different rhetorical techniques, keeping the reader hooked. His use of ethos, logos, and pathos makes his broad audience continue reading and interested in what Pinker has to say about technology. Pinker obviously knows how to write, and write well, but this article showcases his talents with the pen, or in this case, the keyboard.

7

Works Cited

"About." *Steven Pinker*. The President and Fellows of Harvard College, n.d. Web.

6 Sept. 2015.

Pinker, Steven. "Mind Over Mass Media." *The New York Times*. The New York

Times, 10 June 2010. Web. 1 Sept. 2015.

Woollaston, Victoria. "How Often Do You Check Your Phone? The Average Person

Does It 110 times a DAY (and up to Every 6 Seconds in the Evening)." *Mail

Online*. Associated Newspapers, 08 Oct. 2013. Web. 6 Sept. 2015.

Zac Davis

ENG 1001

Professor Richard Shivener

6 September 2014

Texts in Action

TED Talk: How Schools Kill Creativity

Around the world, going to school is a very typical experience for just about all children. Most of us have been there at some point in our lives, going to receive an education through a tedious schedule of academic courses, working our hardest to earn exceptional grades because that is what is expected, isn't it? Ordinarily, academic courses are favored over creativity because those are the skills that are most valued in the world today and have a better chance at landing you a job. We live in a world where the hierarchy of our schools is structured around these academic principles, while we are nudged away from the creative and artistic options such as the ability to play an instrument or craft a work of art. The reason is that creativity has become undervalued in the world today. This is the point made by author and educator Ken Robinson in his TED talk, "How Schools Kill Creativity." In this TED talk given in February of 2006, he argues that schools are structured too academically, and that we should be encouraging creativity to the youth of our world

Davis   2

in order to prepare them for the future. To emphasize his argument, Robinson effectively utilizes rhetorical elements in his speech to make a strong argument, hoping to leave a lasting impact on the audience.

One tool that Robinson uses to entice the audience to make an effective argument is his use of humor. There are a few ways in which he uses this element, whether it is a small joke, or providing comic relief. There are many points throughout his speech where he is telling a story or making a valid point, but at the same time he is making small jokes that make the audience laugh. These little jokes may not always seem like much, but they are actually doing a great job of appealing to the crowd and gaining their attention. Humor is an incredible persuasive tool because it appeals to their emotions, and it makes them feel more comfortable with the speaker. Humor also draws interest toward the speech and the argument, and the attention and trust of the crowd is all Robinson needs in order for him to make his argument effective. One example is a humorous joke that is told by Robinson that actually gives his argument some validity, which is about a girl drawing in school:

I heard a great story recently—I love telling it—of a little girl who was in a drawing lesson. She was six and she was at the back, drawing, and the teacher said this little girl hardly ever paid attention, and in this drawing lesson she did. The teacher was fascinated and she went over to her and she said, "What are you drawing?" And the girl said, "I'm drawing a picture of God." And the teacher said, "But nobody knows what God looks like." And the girl said, "They will in a minute." (Laughter)

These small jokes and stories help develop a respectable human to human relationship between the crowd and Robinson as he speaks at a comfortable level understood by all. Allowing the crowd to become comfortable with Robinson as a speaker is an important piece of the puzzle that allows him to persuade the audience that he is making a credible argument. With the trust and the attention of the crowd at hand, Robinson is able to dig deeper into the issue now that the audience has an idea of where the talk is going, and the farther he burrows in, the larger the impact that he leaves on the audience. Ultimately, this is an essential connection that Robinson makes through his use of humor, as he draws the audience closer to his own argument.

As people begin to consider the speech in respect to their own lives, it does seem true that we have been deprived of creativity. As a child, we all probably had big dreams and enjoyed something that we would've loved to do for the rest of our lives, whether we wanted to be a professional athlete, an artist, a musician, a doctor, or whatever. The list seems to go on and on, but as most of us have grown

Davis   4

up, we have changed our mind, and the reason Robinson points out is that we are told not to. Robinson says that "You were probably steered benignly away from things at school when you were a kid, things you liked, on the grounds that you would never get a job doing that. Is that right? Don't do music, you're not going to be a musician; don't do art, you won't be an artist." The sad thing about this is that it's true, as many of us have been told this at one point in our lives, and it can really tug on the heart strings. Things like this really do impact the crowd and their emotions, which is a great use of pathos.

Pathos remains one of the leading rhetorical strategies used throughout the talk as Robinson transitions to some more bold information. The question that may be on the minds of audience members is how does one lose their creativity through school? In response to this question, Robinson gives a clear-cut answer, which is simply mistakes. As children, we didn't fear being wrong, which is one of the reasons that children happen to be so creative. However, most children have attended a school system where mistakes are one of the worst things you can make. The fact of the matter is that if you are not prepared to be wrong, you will never create anything original from your actions. To finish off this statement, Robinson gives a quote by Picasso which says, "All children are born artists. The problem is to remain an artist as we grow up." These words have an emotional impact on the audience, leaving them to wonder if school really did change who they were creativity-wise, and where they may be in life if they would have approached school without stigmatizing the mistakes. Ultimately, the information used by Robinson throughout the piece plays a crucial role in developing pathos throughout the piece, as the audience gains an emotional understanding from what is presented to them.

When the speech has concluded and Ken Robinson leaves the stage, one may question why they should believe what they listened to and whether or not the argument he made was valid. This is why ethos is so important when trying to convince others to believe an argument, because without any credibility built behind oneself, why should anyone believe you? However, Robinson did do a great job establishing ethos throughout the speech. The fact of the matter is he used to be an educator himself at one point in his life, meaning he is a credible source who understands how a school system runs and the essentials of teaching. You may not want to listen to someone who criticizes school systems around the world if the person had never actually been involved in the matter; however, Robinson's interest and experience in the field of education give him the credibility to express his opinion about schools and the lack of creative options offered to students.

Davis   6

Also, not only was Robinson an educator, but an author wrote a book related to the subject called *The Element: How Finding Your Passion Changes Everything.* This piece of work by Robinson is composed from a number of stories told by people on how they discovered their own special talents. These stories were not about success that was found within the classroom, but rather a success that came from a special talent outside school. As a whole, this book brings to light that there are people out there who struggle in school. But should they be looked down on because of this? Of course not. School wasn't their niche, and instead they found that they were talented in something outside of school which was more creative than anything that was offered to them within an educational environment. Robinson personally collected all of these emotional stories to complete his book, and as author of this piece, he understands that there are people out there who don't always fit in an academic classroom, and that should never be anything to look down on. Ultimately, Robinson is able to use ethos as he asserts his credibility as an educator and an author to help prove that his argument is worth considering given that it is coming from a legitimate source.

By the end of the talk, I strongly believe that Ken Robinson won over the audience and succeeded in convincing them that schools do in fact need to make a change to better prepare the youth of the world for the life ahead of them, a life

where creativity is encouraged. One can see why this is one of the most viewed
TED talks of all time, as the speech is full of humor, memorable stories and quotes,
and strong emotional appeal that has the audience out of their seats applauding by
the end. Ultimately, Ken Robinson performed this speech marvelously, creating a
piece that has left a lasting impact and will inspire for years to come.

Works Cited

Robinson, Ken. "How Schools Kill Creativity." *TED*. Ted.com. Feb. 2006. Web.

 Sept. 6 2014.

Connor Howard

15 September 2015

English 1001 Blewett

"Got Milk?" or "Got Objectification?"

The "Got Milk?" campaign has a reputation of being one of the most well-known campaigns. The aim of the project was to encourage younger people like children and students to drink more milk. First launched in October of 1993, it was mainly comprised of television commercials. The first print ad was released two years later when National Milk Processor Education Program (MilkPREP) bought out the phrase to use on the celebrity ads. The use of famous athletes, actors/actresses, pop stars, and characters both real and fictional (i.e. David Beckham, Britney Spears, Superman) sporting a milk mustache helped the campaign reach its acclaim. In 2007 a print of Hayden Panettiere was released. Featured were a short few lines that read, "You don't have to be a hero to feel invincible. That's why I drink milk. The protein helps build muscle and some studies suggest that teens who choose it tend to be leaner. Cheers to that." In the end, this evolved into a monster of an ad that definitely was not age-appropriate for the community that MilkPREP was targeting as their market.

Howard   2

Panettiere had just turned eighteen-years-old at the time the ad was released. She was starring in the television hit "Heroes" on NBC. She portrayed Claire Bennet, a high school cheerleader with the power of cellular regeneration. Standing a petite 5'0" with naturally blonde hair and a slim build, Panettiere fit the stereotypical mold of her character's description. Those attracted to this ad would most likely have been part of the younger generation, the audience that MilkPREP intended to reach from the beginning. As the company so clearly knew, using a positive household name in an advertisement immediately draws in possible consumers.

There are multiple aspects of the ad that convince viewers to trust this striking young woman. A challenge presented by the use of famous individuals is to make the subject friendly and personable while still holding onto their star quality. Hayden Panettiere was a popular name among young adults and children in the mid- to late-2000's. Her starring role in "Bring It On: All or Nothing" along with her appearances in numerous television commercial advertisements made her familiar in the eyes of the general public, especially those of the younger generation. With this fame in mind, her being pictured makes the person or persons viewing the ad believe that the message Panettiere is promoting is credible. The tacky milk mustache adds a layer of humor and approachability to the print. By evening out the playing field of celebrity versus obscurity MilkPREP has secured a reading of the ad from the viewer(s). The text at the bottom of the ad is also slightly in the character of Claire Bennet. Cleared now are any doubts that Panettiere is indeed portraying her character, Claire Bennet.

In today's society people of all ages are subliminally taught that they need to fit one single mold- white, abled, heterosexual, and male. The ad most definitely takes advantage of this mindset. Panettiere is painted in a way to make women believe they should look like her and make men believe they should want to be with her. Panettiere's slim-fitting red dress immediately captures the eye. With her exceeding society's clíched ideals of beauty, further attention is drawn. The text, however, is what really relates to the viewers' beliefs and values.

The bit about becoming leaner through drinking milk is directed at women. The need to be thin is another idea brought about by society. Sprouting from this is a lack of self-esteem in children which often can lead to depression in later years. Following that is the line that says drinking milk "helps build muscle." It could be argued that this is aimed towards both men and women. In addition to having negative body fat, women are also expected to have a hearty amount of muscle on their bones. Although men don't face nearly as much of this silent bullying as women do, they do face a pressure to be overly muscular. In addition to generally being treated as lesser than men, women are held to higher and much more restrictive expectations of attractiveness.

The logic of this particular advertisement is very much in a grey area. It seems rather nonsensical for Panettiere to be dressed so elegantly while simply drinking milk. One could argue, though, that the lack of a backdrop invites imagination. There are endless possibilities in this mindset. The only blatant flaw in logic is the fact that the milk glass is shattering. There is nothing pictured that explains this, and it isn't related to Claire Bennet's gift in "Heroes" (as previously stated, Bennet's gift is rapid cellular regeneration). While one might say it is a senseless attempt to draw attention, it could be argued that Panettiere's sexuality is such a dominant force that it has in a sense materialized and caused the glass to break.

In short, there are a plethora of aspects that make this quite a despicable ad. Panettiere's body is being exploited solely to promote a product. The only possible explanation for her over-stylized hairdo is the effects milk has on a person's hair, but it still seems excessive. The neckline of her dress is rather revealing, and unnecessarily so. Her bust is the direct center of the photo and immediately below that is her seemingly photoshopped abdomen. The sultry look on her face gives off an aura of intense sexuality. All of these factors pile up into a mess that is completely inappropriate for people in the age range of the desired audience. In this way the

Howard   5

ad is also promoting body-shame and insecurity. The distributors of this ad plan to put them in places that young people frequent. Those young people who don't fit into the unimaginably small percentage of individuals who qualify as "ideal" in society's eyes then believe that this service isn't available to them.

MilkPREP discontinued the "Got Milk?" series in 2014 in lieu of a new catchphrase. Through their over-ten-year run, these ads gained great recognition. By the time it closed, the "Got Milk?" campaign had earned the title of one of the most influential in history. Surprisingly, though, the ads were not as successful as originally planned. Objectification and sexualization is not necessary to sell a product. Everybody knows the marketing saying "sex sells," but as language does, this has became outdated. Taking a living and breathing human and forcing them to be looked at as anything less than that is barbaric and degrading. Panettiere, in addition to countless others, is being stripped of her personality and identity for the pleasure of society.

More respectable "Got Milk?" ads, and perhaps even more successful ones, could have been created if the subjects were all presented as real people rather than just shells of celebrities.

UNIT 2: STUDENT WRITING

Copyright 2017 by Department of English, University of Cincinnati. All rights reserved.

Researched Argument

Making a researched argument is an exciting process that calls for critical reading, analysis, and synthesis. It requires care to bring together several voices in conversation and not lose your own as you seek an answer or solution to the question or problem you pose. It takes even more care to present what you discover in a way that engages readers. In this section, we offer three essays that effectively draw upon the work of others to make compelling arguments.

The first essay, Matthew Dobrilovic's "Nuclear Power for the World," takes on widely held beliefs that nuclear power is dangerous with potentially catastrophic consequences, to argue the contrary: nuclear power is safer, has less environmental impact, and is more economical than other common sources of energy. In the second essay, "Life in a Bathtub," Mattina Girardot draws our attention to the plight of dolphins in captivity. In her impassioned essay, Girardot brings together voices for and against captivity in general, and for and against captivity for scientific research. The final essay by Julia Sharmon "Super Gendered: Hypersexualization and Gender Stereotyping Within the Superhero Industry," examines how superhero films depict male characters as idealized stereotypes of masculinity in impossible-to-attain bodies. Sharmon calls for feminists to turn their attention to desconstructing male superheros along with attending to the overly sexualized representation of female superheros.

Taken as a whole, these essays demonstrate the characteristics of effective researched writing and argumentation: a clearly articulated thesis idea, a logical and signposted structure, carefully intro-duced and cited quotations from credible sources, and attention to other points of view.

Some questions to stimulate discussion about the samples or your own drafts:

- Where does the writer address opposing viewpoints? How does the writer treat other viewpoints? How does discussing others' perspectives affect the persuasiveness of the argument?

- Where does the writer reveal the thesis idea? What are the effects of *where* this statement is revealed? Is the thesis idea clear and debatable?

- How does the writer incorporate research? How does the writer introduce cited research? How does the writer talk about or "unpack" quotations or summaries of research?

- Where do you feel most engaged in the writer's argument? What has the writer done or what moves has the writer made to get your attention? Are you persuaded by the writer's argument? Why or why not?

Matthew Dobrilovic

English 1001

10-26-2015

Nuclear Power for the World

When most people think of nuclear reactors, they may imagine large cooling towers giving off white clouds. They may also remember tragedies in nuclear energy's history such as the partial core melt down at the Three Mile Island power plant, or the even more infamous core melt down at the nuclear reactor in Chernobyl, Russia. Despite the common fear of nuclear power plants being dangerous, the use of nuclear power plants could actually benefit the environment. Nuclear power plants have a minimal environmental impact, provide economic benefits to the local population, and are safer than most other forms of energy.

Many people believe that nuclear power plants have a negative effect on the environment, when in fact they do not. Nuclear power plants actually do not produce much airborne radiation, as explained by nuclear physicists at the Moscow State University: "During normal operation, the influence of NPPs via radioactive air pollution is quite low compared to the natural radioactivity of the atmosphere... "(Gordienko, Brykin, Kuzin, Serebryakov, Starkov, and Tairov 125). From this information, it is clear that nuclear reactors do not produce dangerous

Dobrilovic   2

amounts of airborne radiation as once thought. Nuclear energy can also reduce

the amount of greenhouse gases that lead to global warming. Bryan Walsh, foreign

editor for Time magazine, states that "nuclear [energy] can play a significant role

in decarbonization, but it will only happen if atomic power isn't expensive, all the

more so, given that most of the increase in global energy consumption will be

coming in developing countries that are especially price sensitive." Based on Bryan

Walsh's idea, nuclear reactors, if spread to all countries, could magnify this effect of

decarbonization. Some may argue that decarbonization could be achieved through

the use of solar power, however, as Denver Nicks states that "solar electricity in

Germany will cost almost five times more for every kilowatt hour of electricity it

provides than Finland's new nuclear plant." Denver Nicks' assertion shows that

nuclear energy per kilowatt makes it a logical choice when it comes to the need

for electricity in developing countries. Nuclear power can provide a substantial

amount of energy, at an affordable price, during all conditions unlike renewable

sources such as geothermal, solar, or hydro-electric power.

Through the production of nuclear energy, less nuclear waste is produced

than within a coal fired power plant. In a coal fire power plant, an approximate

288484.747 metric ton of coal waste is produced per year (Environmental Impacts

of Coal Power: Wastes Generated). This number includes the amount of coal ash

Dobrilovic   3

produced from burning the coal as well as the amount of sludge that collects in, and is scraped out of, the smokestack at the plant. In contrast, a nuclear power plant, in the same time span, only produces 20 metric tons of nuclear fuel waste (On-Site Storage of Nuclear Waste).

Minimal waste is not the only advantage that nuclear power has over the conventional thermal powered plant. The Union of Concerned Scientists state that "at least 42 percent of coal combustion waste ponds and landfills are unlined." This is a startling statement to consider, as the waste is just dumped into these ponds and landfills, which causes damage to the local population of wildlife, and may even harm humans if they consume the water. Nuclear waste is often viewed as being dangerous, as it remains radioactive long after it is removed from the reactor. However, most nuclear power plants store the used fuel in man-made "ponds" either at the factory or in an offsite location. In fact, as the World Nuclear Association states, "[p]onds at reactors are often designed to hold all the used fuel for the life of the reactor" (World Nuclear Association). With this system in place for disposing of nuclear material, countries, especially those with limited fresh water supplies, would not have to worry about pollution from a near-by coal fire plant.

Nuclear energy is not only globally beneficial when it comes to the environment, it is also locally and economically beneficial. Nuclear reactors create jobs throughout the life span of the plant: from the construction phase to the daily operation, maintenance, and security of the plant. According to the Nuclear Energy Institute ("NEI), "[n]uclear plants create the largest workforce annual income based on both large capacity and being a labor-intensive technology" ("Nuclear Energy's Economic Benefits"). These economic benefits make nuclear power plants an ideal catalyst for stirring up revenue and providing a sustainable place of employment for the area. Nuclear power plants can also be an abundant source of revenue when it comes to paying taxes. The NEI reports that "The average nuclear plant pays about $16 million in state and local taxes annually. These tax dollars benefit schools, roads and other state and local infrastructure." With the increase in revenue, countries that implement nuclear power will also be giving themselves an economic boost. This boost, as mentioned by the NEI, could be put to good use such as funding improvements in the local school system, allowing more children to obtain an education. Revenue generated from the power plants that go to roads also have larger reaching benefits. As the road infrastructure is improved, the amount of goods that can be shipped via trucks or other ground transportation can be increased, culminating in an increase of the economic situation of those involved directly and indirectly.

Dobrilovic   5

Nuclear energy also has the benefit of providing cheap electricity. Research reported in *Forbes* Magazine, claimed that nuclear energy was the second cheapest form of energy costing only three and a half cents per kilowatt hour (Conca). The low cost of electricity is important because many of today's devices, from electric stoves, to water purifiers, depend on electricity. But nuclear power reaches farther than just local economics. It plays a large role in countries that export supplies for the construction of the power plants and countries that are looking to build and improve their nuclear power infrastructure. With the increase in the need for specific construction materials, the number of orders to export these products has grown. As the Nuclear Energy Institute puts it, "American companies have already booked export orders for billions of dollars in equipment and services, including generators, reactor coolant pumps and instrumentation and control systems" (Nuclear Energy's Economic Benefits). Increases in exports also leads to an increased revenue for the company producing the part, as well as the need for more employees to meet the demand of the global market. The world of nuclear energy creates many jobs and effects millions in a positive way.

However, some might argue that other cleaner sources of energy also produce more jobs and revenue for their area. In fact, renewable energy sources, such as wind, do produce jobs. According to the Union of Concerned Scientist "...

in 2011, the wind energy industry directly employed 75,000 full-time-equivalent employees…" (Benefits of Renewable Energy Use). However, despite this fact, no other form of energy is as efficient as that of nuclear energy. According to the Nuclear Energy Institute, nuclear power plants run at an efficiency of 92 percent, compared to natural gas at 47.8 percent, coal-fire at 60.9 percent, and wind at 33.9 percent (Fact Sheets). These efficiencies are achieved with current technology, and the possibilities are limitless if more countries could be given the opportunity to develop their nuclear programs.

To be sure, there is a fear that some countries may use the enriched uranium to create nuclear weapons that could endanger the peace and safety of those whom may be targeted. These fears can be quelled with a new nuclear reactor that is being developed. This reactor is known as a "molten salt reactor" which uses a form of thorium. Thorium, however, is not the actual fuel, as John H. Kutsch, president of an engineering design consultancy, states: "The thorium is not actually the nuclear fuel. It is converted to the fuel, ^{233}U, when exposed to low-energy neutron". (qtd in Mitch). Using thorium in this way would provide for safer operation pressures and the American Nuclear Society reports Nuclear technology is not perfect, and there are some risks that accompany this type of energy production. A core meltdown or any other number of potential accidents may occur throughout the life of any nuclear reactor. The fear of an accident became a reality on March 28, 1979, when the nuclear power plant in Three Mile Island, Pennsylvania, went into a state of partial nuclear core meltdown. Following this potential catastrophe, "the Pennsylvania Department of Health maintained for 18 years a registry of more than 30,000 people who lived within five miles of Three Mile Island at the time of the accident" (Frequently Asked Questions—Three Mile Island Accident—March 28, 1979). The American Nuclear Society reports that the "state's registry was discontinued in June 1997 without any evidence of unusual health trends" (Frequently Asked Questions—Three Mile Island Accident—March 28, 1979). This feat was achieved due to the built-in safety features of the plant, on top of the ability of the engineering system to cool the reactor to a safe temperature before the situation became any worse. Serious catastrophes such as what occurred at Chernobyl are often thought of as a likely possibility that may occur at a nuclear power plant, despite the fact that this is not the case. The Chernobyl incident was caused due to several factors, which include the inadequate design of the reactor and the lack of safety protocol at the plant. The reports asserts a "peculiarity of the design of the control rods caused a dramatic power surge as they were inserted into the reactor" (Mosey). This factor led to the fuel rods interacting directly with the cooling water, creating an amount of pressure that was too great for the poorly designed reactor.

Dobrilovic   8

Due to modern designs in reactors, it is unlikely that radioactive material would escape the immediate containing vessel. As the World Nuclear Association reaffirms "even if the containment structure that surrounds all modern nuclear plants were ruptured...it is still very effective in preventing escape of most radioactivity"(World Nuclear Association). The implementation of physical safety devices is not the only area in which safety has improved in nuclear power plants. In the wake of the Three Mile Island disaster, safety became an even greater priority throughout American nuclear power plants. After the disaster, the Institute of Nuclear Power Operations was created to ensure that plants were implementing the safest standards. This organization ensures that the "Institute of Nuclear Power Operations promotes high levels of safety and reliability in U.S. nuclear plants by setting performance objectives, criteria and guidelines industrywide for nuclear plant operations, and by conducting regular evaluations of nuclear plants" (Operations Safety). With this air of safety being implemented in power plants, along with the physical safety devices, nuclear energy is marching towards a safer future.

Nuclear energy has a long road to go before it is established and accepted around the world. The potential dangers perceived by the public needs to be balanced with information about nuclear energy's advancing technology and benefits.

Nuclear energy's benefits include reducing the percentage of green-house gases produce when generating electricity, stimulating economies as a result of building and running a nuclear power plant, and employing new technology that makes nuclear energy even safer than previous reactors. As Leslie Dewan, an American entrepreneur, asserts:

> Nuclear power is a young technology—there's so much more to be discovered. That's what makes it so exciting to me. Yes, there are problems, but innovative people are going to be able to come up with solutions and bring the technology to its full potential.

For nuclear energy to truly thrive, it will take the whole world working together to improve this technology, and in turn, improve the lives of millions.

Works Cited

"Benefits of Renewable Energy Use." Union of Concerned Scientists. Union of Concerned Scientists, n.d. Web. 30 Oct. 2015.

Conca, James. "The Naked Cost of Energy—Stripping Away Financing and Subsidies." *Forbes*. Forbes Magazine, 15 June 2012. Web. 30 Oct. 2015.

"Department of Nuclear Safety and Security." Department of Nuclear Safety and Security. International Atomic Energy Agency, n.d. Web. 19 Oct. 2015

Dobrilovic   10

Dewan, Leslie. "Leslie Dewan Quote." BrainyQuote. Xplore, n.d. Web. 30 Oct. 2015.

"Environmental Impacts of Coal Power: Wastes Generated." Union of Concerned Scientists. Union of Concerned Scientists, n.d. Web. 30 Oct. 2015.

"Fact Sheets." Quick Facts: Nuclear Energy in America. Nuclear Energy Institute, July 2015. Web. 30 Oct. 2015.

"Frequently Asked Questions—Three Mile Island Accident—March 28, 1979." ANS / Public Information / Resources / Special Topics / History of Three Mile Island / Frequently Asked Questions. American Nuclear Society, 11 July 2012. Web. 30 Oct. 2015.

Mitch, Jacoby. "Trying to Unleash The Power Of Thorium." *Chemical & Engineering News. Chemical & Engineering News*, 6 July 2015. Web. 10 Oct. 2015

Mosey, David. "World Nuclear Association." Chernobyl. World Nuclear Association, 26 Nov. 2014. Web. 30 Oct. 2015.

Nuclear Energy's Economic Benefits—Current and Future. DC: Nuclear Energy Institute, Apr. 2014. PDF

"Operational Safety." Nuclear Energy Institute. Nuclear Energy Institute, n.d. Web. 09 Nov. 2015.

"On-Site Storage of Nuclear Waste." Nuclear Waste Amounts & On-Site Storage. Nuclear Energy Institute, n.d. Web. 30 Oct. 2015.

Dobrilovic   11

V, Gordienko A., Brykin S. N, Kuzin E. R, Serebryakov S. I, Strakov V. M, and

Tairov N. T. "Nuclear Power Pros and Cons: A Comparative Analysis of Ra-

dioactive Emissions from Nuclear Power Plants and Thermal Power Plants."

Moscow: Moscow University, 4 Oct. 2011. PDF.

Walsh, Bryan. "Nuclear Energy Is Largely Safe. But Can It Be Cheap? | TIME.

com." Science Space Nuclear Energy Is Largely Safe But Can It Be Cheap

Comments. Time Inc., 8 July 2013. Web. 12 Oct. 2015.

"World Nuclear Association." Advanced Nuclear Power Reactors. World Nuclear

Association, May 2015. Web. 19 Oct. 2015.

"World Nuclear Association." Radioactive Waste Management. World Nuclear As-

sociation, Oct. 2015. Web. 30 Oct. 2015.

"World Nuclear Association." Safety of Nuclear Reactors. World Nuclear Associa-

tion, Aug. 2015. Web. 09 Nov. 2015.

Mattina Girardot

Professor Meier

ENGL 1001 – 065

Researched Argument Paper

2 October 2015

Life in a Bathtub

What would you do if you were forced to spend your entire life in a bathtub? Bizarre question, right? It is seemingly farfetched and unrealistic, but this is only because the question is read by a human. Each and every animal in captivity, however, is caged. They may have supposedly "state of the art enclosures" and "plenty of space to live happily," but in reality, there is no way that the wild can be replicated. A dolphin in captivity spends its shortened life in a concrete pool. Many critics of animal rights activities argue that these marine animals are not affected critically by the conditions of captivity. However, research has come to prove and accredit the immense abilities of a dolphin's mind. In light of new discoveries, the conditions and regulations of animal captivity for research vs. entertainment purposes—especially in the case of dolphins—must be readdressed and made known to the public. Before we can claim that animals in captivity are provided for and given a safe and prosperous life, we must ask if spending an entire life in a bathtub would be worth the cost of a lifetime of monotony and boredom.

Extensive research has confirmed the far-reaching mind power of all animals, especially in the case of aquatic mammals. Erik Vance, biologist and writer for *National Geographic* reports on the findings of Dr. Lori Marino, neuroscientist and cetacean expert and a leader in supporting the rights of dolphins, who explains that "pound for pound, dolphins are better endowed with gray matter than most primates, falling just short of humans, and the motor cortex of their brain is just as complex as our own" (1). Although living in different physical and communal environments, dolphins show many similarities to humans: desiring company, understanding complex sentences expressed by human gestures, living as social creatures, functioning as problem solvers, learning the importance of word order, and showing comprehension of self in mirrors (Clemmitt).

As presented by the editors of *Scientific American*, the complexity of problem solving and community are shown in wild orcas (commonly known as "killer whales," but actually a type of dolphin). For example, when orcas are hunting and come across prey, such as seals or penguins on top of icebergs, the orcas will team up with their pods and create organized waves to knock the prey into the water ("Free Willy"). Besides primates, dolphins were the first animals to show self-awareness through experiments involving mirrors. Most animals view mirror images as another being; however, the milestone in animal cognition showed that dolphins are able to recognize themselves, an indication of high levels of intelligence. In the experiment, dolphins with hidden marks on their body contorted to check out their temporary tattoos in mirrors: it was clear that dolphins were more than just a cute source of entertainment (Vance).

Biologist Diana Reiss noticed the potential of dolphins while in Florida exploring her interest in dolphins. A group of dolphins began to play a simple game of fetch with Reiss. After hours of throwing seaweed back and forth with the dolphins, Reiss understood, that "there is someone in there. It's not a human, but it is someone" (qtd. in Vance 3). In another study, Dr. Louis Herman, professor of psychology at the University of Hawaii and founder of a research-only dolphin facility in Honolulu in 1970, along with her co-researchers identified the comprehension of word order in dolphins with the female bottle-nosed dolphin named Akeakamai. Herman and her co-researchers saw that Akeakamai was able to understand the sign language that indicated objects and locations, such as right and left. Akeakamai would bring a surfboard to her trainer when told "person surfboard fetch," and when told "surfboard person fetch," Akeakamai would push her trainer to the surfboard instead, showing her grasp of varied word orders (Herman).

Girardot   4

The research exploring the high level of intelligence in dolphins is causing the treatment of dolphins to be evaluated in an ethical and moral manner. Clemmitt observes another astonishing capability possessed by dolphins; they are able to:

Use echolocation to navigate their underwater environment, bouncing sound waves off objects in front of them. This mode of perception is so precise that a dolphin can locate a piece of metal buried in two feet of mud and tell trainers whether the metal is brass or stainless steel.

Underwater, dolphins rely on their echolocation, but above water, they are able to use their sonar sense to recognize objects by translating it to an actual visual. In the 1960s the U.S. Navy used this dolphin skill when it began training and using dolphins to retrieve practice rockets and mines that ended up on the ocean floor (Grimm 527). Although the Navy's work with dolphins led to advances in dolphin research, we might ask whether training these intelligent animals for militaristic purposes was an abusive use of their ability to swim and recognize objects. Of course, they can swim better and longer than human divers, but are these animals being treated properly? They are replacing a human's job; however, are they being treated like a hardworking and trained human?

But more troubling than dolphins being used for military purposes is the abuse they are subjected to as tourist attractions due to their endearing and sociable

Girardot   5

appearance. Sharanya Prasad, US Programs Manager for the World Society for the Protection of Animals, writes that the adorable "smile" that visitors love, is simply the shape of the dolphins' mouths and shows no connection to their emotional status. All around the world, dolphins—particularly bottlenose and orca—are used as tourist attractions in choreographed shows. But the supposed "close bond" between trainer and animal reveals an underlying assumption of mastery over the cetaceans, as if humans believe they are better than the animals in their care. Professor of Animal Welfare at the University of Queensland in Australia, Clive Phillips, deplores the use of animals in shows by explaining:

The animals are portrayed as apparently enjoying the interactions with their trainer and with the audience. The reward for them is simply food, with little or no evidence that they find the interactions entertaining. In fact, the restricted autonomy and poor welfare that they are forced to endure leads to occasional hostile interactions with trainers and even rare deaths. Some of the worst incidents are well publicized, as anyone who has seen the 2013 documentary film Blackfish about the welfare of killer whales in captivity will be well aware of. An ethical analysis might conclude that humans have taken advantage of these animals' natural curiosity, which functions to give them an ecological advantage in the wild.

Girardot   6

Due to the growth of captive dolphin attractions, there is a demand through-out the world for live dolphins. Prasad testifies that the high demand cannot be met by breeding captive dolphins; therefore, they are drawn from the wild pop-ulations. Japan, in particular, Prasad points out, is known for its brutally bloody dolphin hunts. She writes that more dolphins than necessary are caught, and those not chosen for live sale are killed, butchered for their meat. Even those dolphins sold in the live sale do not have a high probability of surviving, Prasad reports: 53% end up dying before 3 months of captivity. The trauma of being hunted is another leading cause of death in captured dolphins (Prasad).

Any minimally ethical observer can see the level of wrongdoing and cruelty that is occurring throughout the world. Even though dolphins are in fact different than humans, they do not deserve less respect. Keeping these differences in mind, there is also proof of similarities between humans and dolphins in aspects of our in-tellectual and emotional states. At least, this fact should influence a new look into the ethics of holding these animals captive. Humans have a responsibility to wild animals. Whether this means releasing all captive dolphins, stopping the capture of wild dolphins, ceasing the use of dolphins in entertainment, or allowing only captive dolphins for the use of research in sufficient wild replicated facilities, there is no definite answer at this time. The issue needs to be brought out as a priority. It is true that human biases make this topic difficult for humans to interpret the facts from emotions, but that does not negate the significance of the rights that these intelligent animals should be given. Dr. Marino asks, "[i]f dolphins were as self-aware as people… how can we keep them locked up in concrete pens?"

The supporters of zoos and aquariums defend their dedication to wildlife conservation and animal prosperity. Wildlife conservation and attempts to understand animals more clearly are amazing goals; however, these are not the sole purposes of most zoos and aquariums. They are used as tourist attractions and money makers. If this were not true, there would be no dolphin and killer whale shows and no animals kept in mediocre enclosures. The main attention of the owners would be to showcase these majestic animals in displays as close to the wild as possible and as big as space allows. If an enclosure is not big enough for an animal, tough decisions should be made about what needs to be adjusted and sacrificed to assure that dolphins have the best life that they can while in captivity.

Conservationist and zoologist Dr. Michael Hutchins explains that "raising public awareness about endangered species and other environmental issues is an important aspect of conservation" (961–962). There is no argument against this necessity; however, zoos and aquariums should not "raise awareness" through

Girardot   8

animal shows. Zoos and aquariums should instead, Hutchins argues, serve as ed-

ucational facilities only. This, of course, is a major shift in the traditional idea of a

zoo and will take some time to gain public acceptance, but in the long run, a little

patience is worth it to protect the natural rights of others.

Dr. Marino has also exposed false claims that have been made by those who

believe it hypocritical to advocate against showing dolphins in aquariums while

supporting scientific research on dolphins. In a letter to the editor of *Science Mag-

azine*, Marino clarifies that although,

Menard [the former executive director of the Alliance of Marine Mammal

Parks and Aquariums] claims that the research we propose with lone, sociable,

and habituated wild dolphins would be prohibited under the Marine Mammal

Protection Act … MMPA prohibits harassment and feeding of wild dolphins but

provides permits for scientific research. (405)

She also addresses Menards's assertion that dolphins live twice as long in cap-

tivity as compared to the wild, claiming that captivity lengthens rather than short-

ens lives. The papers cited by Menard, Marino claims, do not support his state-

ments and make no comparison between wild and captive dolphin life spans, only

the life stages and growth of wild dolphins (405).

Girardot   9

Unlike Marino, many scientists shy away from supporting the rights of animals in such strong, opinionated ways. This is sadly due to the fact that scientists' reputations are easily polluted from public activism. It shows that the researcher has an opinion and can be subjective in situations—anathema to scientific "objectivity"—thereby invalidating research. Vance shares that after viewing a film showing the hunting of dolphins off the coast of Japan at a high profile annual meeting of the American Association for the Advancement of Science, "one scientist stood and declared in a huff that activism had no place in science. But others lingered for hours, discussing the concept that dolphins were people—not quite like us, but people all the same" (Vance). Although some scientists stick to their classical ways of anti-activism, most saw the wrong in the issue, and voluntarily risked tainting their credibility by showing their support of the rights of dolphins.

One of the major concerns of dolphin activists are the conditions in which captive dolphins exist. Dolphins normally swim up to 50 miles daily. This is physically impossible for captive dolphins, resulting in aimless circular swimming out of boredom in what feels like a bathtub to them. The editors of *Scientific American* suggest that confinement drives cetaceans into psychotic behaviors. The stresses of captivity cause unnatural behaviors and as a result, premature dolphin deaths ("Free Willy" 10). One horrific example is cited by David Grimm who reported that Harley—a bottlenose dolphin in the Minnesota Zoo—had his life cut short in January of 2006, by jumping out of his pool and smacking his head on the concrete around the pool. Harley was returned to his pool when his trainers assumed no harm was done (Grimm 526). Soon, having stopped coming up for air, Harley died from a fractured skull before divers could save him (Grimm 526).

Dolphins deserve entire oceans as their playgrounds and endless interactions with hundreds of pod mates. Humans have no right to inflict such physical and psychological damage on the beautiful and intelligent dolphins of the world.

Works Cited

Clemmitt, Marcia. "Animal Intelligence." *CQ Researcher*. CQ Press, 22 Oct. 2010. Web. 28 Oct. 2015.

"Free Willy—And All His Pals." *Scientific American* 310.3 (2014): 10. *Academic Search Complete*. Web. 28 Nov. 2015.

Grimm, David. "Are Dolphins Too Smart For Captivity?" *Science* 332.6029 (2011): 526-529. *Academic Search Complete*. Web. 28 Oct. 2015.

Herman, Louis M. "Language Learning." *The Dolphin Institute Resource Guide*. The Dolphin Institute, n.d. Web. 28 Oct. 2015.

Girardot   11

Hutchins, Michael, Brandie Smith, and Ruth Allard. "In Defense Of Zoos And
    Aquariums: The Ethical Basis For Keeping Wild Animals In Captivity." *Journal of the American Veterinary Medical Association* 223.7 (2003): 958-966. *Academic Search Complete*. Web. 28 Oct. 2015.

Marino, Lori. "Dolphin Research: Arguing Against Captivity." *Science* 333.6041
    (2011): 405. *Academic Search Complete*. Web. 1 Nov. 2015.

Phillips, Clive. "A Whale of a Problem." *Australian Geographic* 120 (2014): 37.
    Academic Search Complete. Web. 28 Oct. 2015.

Prasad, Sharanya "Con" in "Pro/Con: Can live dolphin exhibits help protect this
    intelligent species?" *CQ Researcher*. CQ Press, 22 Oct. 2010. Web. 28 Oct.
    2015.

Vance, Erik. "Dolphin Desperadoes." *Discover* 32.7 (2011): 62-74. *Academic
    Search Complete*. Web. 7 Oct. 2015.

Julia Sharman

Dr. Kay

English 1001

April 23, 2015

Super Gendered: Hypersexualization and Gender Stereotyping

Within the Superhero Industry

Take a moment and picture a superhero. Imagine someone who fights evil, res-

cues civilians, and saves the day. What does this person look like? More than likely,

you pictured someone who perfectly embodies gender roles and stereotypes. If you

pictured a male superhero, he probably had nice hair, a straight jawline, muscles,

and a dashing smile. However, if you pictured a female superhero then she likely

had a nice figure, revealing clothes, and beautiful locks. This comes as no surprise

because a majority of the superheroes fit neatly into two boxes we label either

male or female. While both superheroes and heroines exemplify traditional gender

stereotypes, the main focus and outrage over these stereotypes tends to be geared

towards the latter. The conversation currently happening around superheroes is

mostly about how female superheroes are portrayed. While this conversation is

vital and in no way should its importance be diminished, if feminism pursues gen-

der equality, then it needs to deconstruct gender roles for men as well as women.

Sharman   2

This means that it is important to identify and discuss the problems with the ways both male and female superheroes are portrayed. Gender plays a massive role in superhero identity and despite popular belief, both male and female superheroes fall victim to the hypersexual, hypermasculine, gender-stereotypical fantasy that exists in the superhero industry.

In recent years, superhero films have become a huge aspect of American pop culture. People who would never read comic books are sporting Superman shirts and waiting in line at theaters to see the latest Avengers movie. But before superheroes were considered "mainstream," there had been a loyal comic book fan base for years. Because of America's long history with superheroes, it would be logical to say that superheros represent the ideals and values of our culture. As Mervi Miettinen from the University of Tampere puts it, "...the superhero usually embodies the tough, uncompromising, masculine virtues of the American nation..." (105). A huge indicator of this perspective would be the way superheroes exhibit their masculinity. One way to define masculinity is, "a set of expectations that society deems appropriate for a male subject to exhibit" (Gates 28) and Americans definitely have very clear rules about how men should look and act. Miettinen points out that in the case of the male superhero, "the essential masculine attributes attached to him stress the ideal as white, heterosexual, muscular, and violent." (105). The superhero

Sharman   3

industry has created an archetype for male characters that are meant to represent the ideal man's appearance, sexuality, characteristics, physical behaviors, and attitude. From the classic Superman movie to newer ones such as *Iron Man,* each male superhero somehow embodies the "perfect" American man.

One of the main, and more obvious, aspects of superhero masculinity is appearance. From brawny muscles to chiseled chins, appearance plays an important part in how superheroes are viewed. The male superhero's appearance is often hypersexual and hypermasculine. In an analysis of the embodiment of superheroes, Dr. Edward Avery-Natale suggests that "[w]hile female characters are fetishized through their breasts, thighs, hair, and lips, the fetish of the male characters is singular in the portrayal of male power through exaggerated musculature" (80). A muscular appearance is so important that often the actors who play superheroes have to work out rigorously in order to achieve that figure. For example, before actor Chris Pratt was the handsome, fit Star Lord in *Guardians of the Galaxy*, he played goofy, chubby Andy Dwyer on *Parks and Recreation*. In order to prepare for his new role, Pratt lost 60 pounds in six months (Weisman).

Hollywood expects a lot from its actors because it understands how central appearance is to superhero characters. Captain America is another example of how important muscles are to the male superhero. In the films, Chris Evans plays Steve

Rogers who is eager to join the military in order to fight in World War II. Unfortunately, Rogers is rejected multiple times due to his small size and weak health. This changes when he is given a serum that completely changes his physique, turning him into a Super Soldier. Performing at the maximum human potential, Captain America becomes an American icon, defeats evil, and saves the human race (*Captain America*). This story exemplifies a common idea of masculinity because before he had muscles, Steve Rogers wasn't good enough. It wasn't until after his transformation that people took notice of him and he became a leader. As Captain America, he became an American icon and represented the strength of his country. In his story, Captain America provides the people with a brawny, clean-cut, all-American hero to believe in. Whether it's the actor playing the hero or the character himself, a muscular body can be the difference between being a less-than-average guy to being a superhero.

Another big distinction of stereotyped masculinity is character traits and attitude. A society with very specific gender roles expects men are to be tough, courageous, and leader-like. These stereotypical characteristics are heavily emphasized in male superheroes. When Dr. Avery-Natale analyzed superheroes in DC Comics, he came across a scenario in which Superman's alter ego, Clark Kent, refuses to fight a bully and is consequently seen as cowardly and "less masculine" by his

Sharman   5

love interest. Avery-Natale later goes on to say, "Superman, for example, is the 'real man,' while Clark Kent is 'less than' a man, as he is not only weak but also a coward and a pacifist" (92–93). While you would expect any superhero, male or female, to be tough, that trait is much more stressed in male superheroes. In a study that focused on gender-role stereotyping of superheroes, researchers found, "males tended to be portrayed as more aggressive and constructive than females, whereas females were more likely to be portrayed as deferent" (Baker and Raney 26). Within group settings such as the Justice League or the Avengers, a majority of the time, the males take charge, make decisions, and find solutions. Although there are no official leadership positions, it is clear to fans that Batman and Superman lead the Justice League while the Avengers are led by Captain America and Tony Stark. These leadership characteristics coincide perfectly with ideas about gender roles and stereotypes and how society expects a man to behave.

Another characteristic that seems to be inherent in many male superheroes is success and power. An obvious reason for the prevalence of this trait is the gender stereotype that men should be successful. We expect men to succeed and to hold powerful positions. Although not every male superhero is highly successful, success does seem to be a common characteristic. Two of the most obvious examples of successful superheroes are Batman and Iron Man. Both are billionaires who use their money to obtain power, and power is essential to their identity. Without his money, Tony Stark would not be Iron Man; his intelligence and success allows him to create a suit that gives him remarkable ability. While Batman's physical abilities are due to training and dedication, Bruce Wayne uses his money to create the Batsuit and the Batcave. His money also gives him great power and influence within the city of Gotham. The power that Batman and Tony Stark possess results in civilians not only trusting them, but even celebrating them.

In addition to the hero worship that accompanies the superheroes' success, in the superhero universe, even organizations allow superheroes to gain power within the government. For example, the Mutant Academy from X-Men trains mutants and gives them authority and power they would otherwise lack. The organization S.H.I.E.L.D. exemplifies those same ideas. Superheroes who are enlisted in these programs have incredible technology at their disposal and are trusted with highly classified missions. On the other side of the spectrum, it seems that a lower-to-middle-class superhero like Spiderman must work much harder to earn the trust of his city. Without wealth or a powerful organization to back him up, Spiderman must rely solely on his skill to prove that he is a hero who can keep his city safe. In the stereotyped world of the superhero, Spiderman might be considered less masculine than Batman or Iron man because he lacks the wealth and power that male gender stereotypes call for.

Sharman 7

Although it seems obvious that male superheroes are equal sufferers when it comes to hypersexualization, they are often left out of the conversation. The feminist outcry is focused solely on female superheroes. And despite their eagerness to point out the flaws within the genre, there has been no discussion about the underlying problem; the same notion of "ideal" masculinity that has molded male superheroes also plays a prominent role in the creation of female superheroes. It is no secret that the superhero industry is male-dominated and that the male perspective has influenced the making of female superheroes. The way female characters look and act is mainly geared toward a male audience.

Only recently have women begun to participate in the superhero genre as writers and audience members. Because there was a lack of women in the industry, female superheroes have traditionally been being created by men, for men. In a critical essay, author Sabine Lebel quotes Scott Bukatman:

Hypermasculine fantasy is also revealed, with unabashed obviousness, in the approach to female superheroes. The spectacle of the female body in these titles is so insistent and the fetishism of breasts, thigh, and hair is so complete, that the comics seem to dare you to say anything about them that isn't just redundant. Of course, the female form has absurdly exaggerated sexual characteristics; of course, the costumes are skimpier than one could (or should) imagine; of course there's no

Sharman   8

visible way that these costumes could stay in place; of course, these women represent simple adolescent masturbatory fantasies (with a healthy taste of dominatrix). (56)

When creating female characters, writers are keeping in mind the fantasies of their male—and mainly, young male—audience. This sexualization of female superheroes has become inherent to the characters themselves. The same way muscles are important to male superheroes, breast size seems to be just as important to female characters. It is so essential, in fact, that when a female creator suggested drawing smaller, more realistic breasts, she was turned down by her editors (Avery-Natale 75). This is because female superheroes aren't meant to look realistic, they are meant (and expected) to look like women from male fantasies.

The substantial amount of hypersexuality, hypermasculinity, and heteronormativity that exists within the superhero industry is reflective of the culture that created it. Superheroes are constantly being remade, but hypersexualization still remains. This is because gender is at the core of superhero identity. For male superheroes, that means expressing an ideal sense of masculinity. As for female superheroes, that means fitting into an ideal of femininity that stems from a male audience. Superheroes have been around for years and with the rise in popularity, it does not appear that they will be going anywhere anytime soon. As a result, creators have a

Sharman   9

great amount of power and opportunity to take this influential genre and make it much more inclusive.

Recently, for example, Marvel comics introduced Ms. Marvel, a "teen Muslim shape-shifter" and has given X-Woman, Storm, a monthly book (Weinman 60). Storm and Ms. Marvel prove that it is possible to change the way superheroes are presented in a way that is modern and that encompasses a growing fan base. To truly empower and represent fans of the superhero genre, creators need to reevaluate what it means to be a superhero. Furthermore, if feminist fans want to establish themselves within the genre, they need to care about how gender itself is being represented, both male and female. After all, both genders succumb to the fantasies that exist within the superhero industry.

Work Cited

Avery-Natale, Edward. "An analysis of emobiment among six superheroes in DC comics." *Social Thought & Research* 2013: 71-106. *SocINDEX.* Web. 9 Feb. 2015.

Baker, Kaysee and Raney, Arthur A. "Equally Super?: Gender-Role Stereotyping of Superheroes In Children's Animated Programs." *Mass Communication & Society* 2007: 25-41. *Communication & Mass Media Complete.* Web. 9 Feb. 2015.

Sharman   10

Captain America: The First Avenger. Dir. Joe Johnston. Perf. Chris Evans. Marvel Studios, 2011. Film.

Gates, Philippa. *Detecting Men: Masculinity and the Hollywood Detective Film*. Albany: State University of New York Press, 2006. Web. 11 Mar. 2015.

Lebel, Sabine. "Turn Down the Boobs, Please!" *CineAction* 77 (2009): 56+. *Expanded Academic ASAP*. Web. 9 Feb. 2015.

Miettinen, Mervi. "Men of Steel? Rorschach, Theweleit, and Watchmen's Deconstructed Masculinity." *PS, Political Science & Politics* 47.1 (2014): 104-7. *ProQuest*. Web. 11 Mar. 2015.

Weinman, Jamie J. "Who's afraid of Wonder Woman? Unlike in the comics business, Hollywood is still reluctant to give a female superhero the starring role." *Maclean's* 2014: 60+. *Expanded Academic ASAP*. Web. 9 Feb. 2015.

Weisman, Aly. "Here's How Chris Pratt Got Ripped For Marvel's 'Guardians Of The Galaxy' *Business Insider*. 1 Aug. 2014. Web. 12 Mar. 2015.

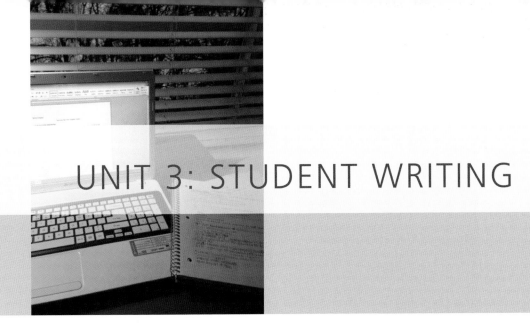

UNIT 3: STUDENT WRITING

Recasting for a Public Audience

The recast involves translating the argument in your research essay into a different medium tailored to a specific audience, purpose, and context. Your instructor may provide you with a specific genre, purpose, or audience for this assignment, but every recast requires you to present your argument in a public form.

So that you can elaborate on the choices you made in recasting your researched argument, you'll also write a rationale. You can think of the rationale as a kind of artist's statement of your work, as a chance to explain your choices and to reflect upon their intended effects.

This section features recast rationales from Alison Arnone, Matthew Dobrilovic, and Greyson Marks. Alison, Matthew, and Greyson each chose to recast their researched arguments in a digital form. You can find Alison's billboard with its link to the website she created, and Matthew's and Greyson's videos in the e-book.

Some questions to stimulate discussion, of the samples or your own recasts:

- Refer back to Matthew's argument essay, "Nuclear Power for the World," in the sample researched argument section. What elements of his research essay appear in his recast? What argument does he feature in his video? How does he appeal to his audience in the written argument and in the video?

- How do issues of copyright appear in the recasts and how are they addressed in the rationales? How does the criteria of Fair Use apply to these recasts?

- How do the writers address their choice of medium, purpose, context, and audience in the recast rationales?

- How does each writer's ethos come across in the recasts and rationales? How do they demonstrate credibility and expertise?

- Choose one of the sample recasts and discuss what other possible choices the writer could have made: what would be the effect of a different choice of medium, purpose, context, or audience?

View Alison's full project at http://wpaindustryimpact.weebly.com/

Alison Arnone

Professor Nordgren

English Composition 1001

16 November 2015

Recast Rationale for "Polluted Pennsylvania"

When I was considering a medium to recast my researched argument about the pollution caused by the steel and natural gas industries in Pittsburgh, I wanted to make use a visual one because I believe being able to see something is an effective way to get an audience's attention on a topic. With that idea in mind, I decided to create a virtual billboard; however, my four years of classes of Photoshop didn't prepare me for how difficult it would be to recast my paper into a picture that is supposed to tell people about how the steel and natural gas industries destroyed the environment. Luckily, my paper had many different options to choose from, but actually executing the options was a difficult task. I chose to represent the dangers of industry to water supplies in the western Pennsylvanian region by including pictures that were taken during the peak of the industries in Pittsburgh. After completing my billboard, I decided to make it more realistic and include more information by creating a website with the included on the billboard.

Rhetorical appeals and strategies used in the billboard include pathos and ethos. In my research paper, I tried to show my credibility, my ethos, through incorporating facts and statistics from sources. I wanted to have my billboard look credible, too, but I used ethos in a different way than I did in my paper. Instead of stating facts and citing sources, the billboard uses historical pictures, asks a question, and provides a website to establishes credibility. Asking a question and providing a website shows that as a rhetor, I know the answer to the question and can provide that information to the audience.

I intended the question and historical photo as an appeal to emotion or pathos. The question makes the audience think about what they know. The images showing actual events make the audience assume that the answer to the question on the billboard is in the pictures. The pictures show Pittsburgh when smoke and soot was always in the sky and the rivers were constantly polluted. By including these images, I wanted the audience to assume that the water in question is shown in the pictures. That assumption plays with the audiences' emotions by influencing them to believe and support the argument of my research paper. The website's purpose is mainly to provide more information and lend more credibility.

The targeted audience of the billboard is citizens of Pittsburgh and anyone who commutes, so the ideal location of the billboard would be on the side of one

Arnone   3

of the major highways going into the city. Making a public display that is visible to many assumes that a large number of people will see it. The website's intended audience would be those who visit the link on the billboard, but it might have traffic from anyone researching the topic and coming across my website.

Billboards have the potential of being very effective if designed well, but they take time and a lot of brainstorming to be very effective. I unfortunately found this out the hard way when I made about five potential billboards. After many hours of Photoshop, I settled on my final one because it displayed my argument the best. Billboards are effective because they are able to show an argument in a very direct way, yet they leave interpretation up to the audience. If drivers drove past my billboard, in the very few seconds that they would see it, they could see that I am arguing that the water in Pittsburgh is polluted. But unless they followed the link and researched more about the topic, they probably wouldn't know about my whole argument: that industry has negatively impacted the environment in the Western Pennsylvanian Region. Websites tend to be very effective in making an argument because of all the information they are able to include. Having a lot of information on a billboard is very difficult because the amount of time spent looking at it is very small.

Arnone   4

As I finish this project, I have a new appreciation for billboard and even poster designers. Photoshop is not an easy tool to use; however, I did enjoy messing with the different features to make the billboard as realistic as possible. I spent a decent amount of time searching for pictures that were both effective and clear. Many pictures on Google were very small and made the billboard very blurry and pixelated. As I said before, I tried many different ideas but none of them looked right because I had no set plan. That is when I went to the good old-fashioned paper, pencil, and markers. After I drew out my ideas, I was able to choose the best idea and execute it well on Photoshop using the hard copy I made.

I noticed that most billboards have links to websites, which is why I also created a website. The information used in the website came from the websites I used in my research paper. Overall, I enjoyed the assignment and the opportunity to use different mediums from those I used in former English classes.

Dobrilovic

Matthew Dobrilovic

English 1001

Ms. Doyle

11-27-2015

Link to recast video: https://youtu.be/wuFwzxwS77I

Recast Rationale for "Nuclear Power for the World"

For the recast project of my argument essay, "Nuclear Power for the World," I decided to make a short video to convey the points that I laid out in my research. The purpose of this video was not to try and sway viewers' opinions through the use of logic as I did in my research paper, but to address a few points discussed in my paper in a visual form. Reformatting my paper into a video allowed me to reach my intended audience, college-age consumers of videos posted on YouTube.

The purpose of my recast was to take a serious topic, nuclear power for all countries, and make a fun video that does not seem as though I am forcing an idea onto the audience. This was an important aspect that I had to consider: if a video pushes an idea too much, then it can have a negative effect, turning people away from the ideas presented. When creating my video, I worked to make the idea obvious enough throughout the dialogue, but kept the video entertaining so that

Dobrilovic   2

I could guide the audience to reach my intended conclusion: that nuclear energy is safe.

Because my paper was somewhat technical with its discussion about specific environmental impacts and new technologies in nuclear energy development, I needed to make the technical more appealing to my audience, so I decided to incorporate humor. Humor is an integral part in making a video that will be shared and remembered among the college-age viewers I wanted to attract. I included humorous dialogue in a familiar newscast form to capture and hold the attention of my audience. The video includes a comment section so that I can interact with those who comment on the video.

Throughout my video I used and recombined some known clichés from other videos. One is the use of a newscaster narrating the disasters that are going on at that time. I borrowed another trope from the horror movie genre: the main character waking up from a dream to realize everything is ok. I like seeing familiar aspects in videos, so I incorporated these clichés as a means to keep my audience's attention. The inclusion of these familiar shots is also timely and current because there are a plethora of movies that use these tropes. I decided to incorporate other effects into the video such as the lights flickering and the monsters appearing as a way to add suspense, keep the video interesting, and hold the audience's attention.

Dobrilovic   3

Creating and editing the video was a difficult and time-consuming process, but also a rewarding one that allowed me to portray my idea in a visual manner. With the visual recast of my research, I was able to tailor the more academic topic of nuclear power into a more interesting form to appeal to my audience. I hope viewers share my video so that it might influence others about the topic of nuclear energy.

Greyson Marks

English Comp 1001

Ms. Blewett

November 24, 2015

Link to Recast Project: https://www.youtube.com/watch?v=OthcUJYWrEM

Can Sweatshops be Good?

My intended audience for my persuasive, informational video about sweatshop labor is anyone who watches videos on YouTube. Nowadays, putting a video on YouTube is just as effective in reaching an audience as it is putting something on the morning TV news or on the radio. Videos reach everyone, especially if they're popular and go viral, and unlike the morning news, anyone can watch videos anywhere at any time.

I intended my video to introduce a new side of the argument of sweatshops, one that not many think of or hear about because they only know what is on TV commercials about how people in sweatshops are abused and why sweatshops should be abolished. My video attempts to persuade viewers that sweatshops can be good because the pay makes workers better off than they would be in most other jobs that they can choose from. I attempt to enlighten those who think that all

Marks   2

sweatshops are bad to help them understand that sweatshops should not be abolished and that they are actually good and necessary.

My recast is a persuasive, informational video. I thought that a video would be a big hit with everyone, and my thoughts were later proven correct when I proposed it to my classmates and they all were very excited to see it. Although my classmates said they were excited, they probably didn't know that I have had experience with making videos, so I didn't think they expected much, which made me more determined to make my video even better and surprise everyone.

Except for my voice, I decided not to include myself in the video; instead, I use clips and pictures that I hope help the audience better understand my perspective and keep them interested. I use many pictures to tell stories and show examples to help convey my opinion. I also use a lot of animation, which is something I had not done before, so it was difficult, but fun, to try.

The topic about the value of sweatshops is a bit hard to take on since it goes against what most people believe about such a controversial subject. My side of the argument is not a popular one, so it was hard to create a situation that would catch the attention of those who think sweatshops are bad, and that was my biggest challenge in doing this recast. Many might think that I am wrong to think that

Marks   3

sweatshops are good, or that like the big CEOs, I only care about money, but that's not true. I believe that sweatshops are bad, too, but I don't believe that they should be abolished because if you abolish sweatshops, the workers would be without jobs. There aren't many jobs available for unskilled workers, if there are jobs where the workers live at all, and the ones they can get, pay a lot less than a sweatshop job. Sweatshop jobs pay close to minimum wage or wages set for standards of living, so sweatshop jobs are actually a better choice for them. People who work in sweatshops often don't have a lot of choices, and a job in a sweatshop might be the only alternative to no job at all.

UNIT 4: STUDENT WRITING

Reflecting on Your Work

Reflection is a skill central to your development as a writer and thinker. In this section, we feature reflective essays by Tyler Creel and Thomas Dzierzak along with a visual reflection by Hannah Thomas.

Your instructor may ask you to produce a different genre or structure for this assignment, but every reflection should consider, weigh, and evaluate specific experiences in ENGL 1001.

The sample pieces do many things your instructor may ask you to do: consider what you've learned and how you've grown in ENGL 1001, examine specific difficulties and successes in performing the composing tasks of ENGL 1001, and imagine how your experiences in ENGL 1001 might carry over to future writing situations.

Some questions to stimulate discussion of the samples or your own drafts:

- How does the composer demonstrate and discuss what has been learned in the course?

- Does the composer make an *argument*? Is the act of reflecting the same or different from making an argument? How is the composer persuasive?

- How does the composer use specific examples as evidence of learning or growth?

- What is the structure of the reflection? How does the writer move from one concept or idea to the next?

Copyright © 2017 by University of Cincinnati, for all student essays. All rights reserved.

Reflection Paper

Tyler Creel

Professor Boehr

1 December 2015

It seems crazy to be already looking back and reflecting on an entire fifteen weeks of class. I feel like it was only the other day that I was walking into the classroom for the first time. Over this past semester, I have learned so much about the composition of writing, but also a lot about myself as a person. In high school I was never the person who was excited when I had to write a paper for something, but after going through this class, I have gained a new appreciation for what goes into a paper in order for it to qualify as good writing.

Throughout this course, I have learned a lot about myself as a writer that I wasn't expecting to. Through the writing I did in this course, I realized that I am a person who has to re-read my paper several times before it starts to sound good. When I write my paper initially, I try and make sure that all the thoughts I have in my head are put onto paper in some form. I have a tendency to wait until the last moment to do my papers, so I do not always have the most time to look them over and revise them, but I have come to the conclusion that this is what I need the most. I also realize that I am very vague when I write. This is not a good habit, and

I improved significantly by writing everything in this course. My writing practices have definitely changed, and will remain changed, especially after doing the research paper. If I hadn't taken this course and were about to write a research paper, I would have just started writing and found information and sources as I went. After writing the paper in this course, I see the benefits of doing multiple research steps: it really helps you lay out what you are writing about and makes the entire writing process much simpler. There are some patterns that I can identify from the way I approached my first paper, the Texts in Action, as compared to our last research paper. For the Texts in Action paper, I was unclear the entire time about the end goal. Due to that, I did not put my determination or any motivation behind the assignment; I simply tried to get it done. After I turned the paper in for the first time, I did not get the grade I wanted, so I put in the time to get a better grade and get through the project. In comparison, the research paper, for the most part, has been enjoyable for me. It has taken up a lot of my time, but my topic revolves around something I am particularly interested in, and because of that, I have more motivation to look deeper and make it a quality paper. I am not exactly sure if it was due to the lack of understanding in the first paper or the increased passion about the second one that made me approach them differently, but I am confident that both of the papers I created are noteworthy.

Creel   3

Another type of knowledge gained throughout this course was about the actual content itself. While I learned multiple concepts, there was one that really stuck out to me because it was something that I had not really paid much attention to in the past. Looking at things from different perspectives can be difficult for some people but is very vital to producing a great piece of writing. Although this was at times difficult to do, it taught me a lot about the subject I was working with. Regardless of who you are, everyone has an opinion or takes a stance on something. This is what makes it hard because when you look through alternative viewpoints, you have to put aside everything you know and think on a completely different side of the spectrum. The biggest thing I learned from looking from different viewpoints was how to build strong support for my side of the argument. Since you are looking at both sides, you can identify where the weaknesses are of the point you are trying to make, and from that, build a stronger case or find the needed evidence to counter the argument. This is important when you are trying to write a persuasive piece because as the writer you know that there are going to be people who agree and disagree with you. The people who disagree with you are going to try their hardest to find a weak point in your argument where they can make a good point that makes the opposing side look stronger. Looking through different perspectives allows for you to make sure they cannot do that to your argument

Creel   4

because you have thought things out from all sides. Once I finally understood how this process was to be done, writing became much easier for me and I felt that my writing was better than ever. This is something that I am going to use on a daily basis, even outside of writing to make myself better.

Rhetorical knowledge is another piece that I learned a lot about that I never strongly considered in writing before. The whole idea of looking at things from different perspectives can be better understood if you know your purpose and audience. Being the author of a piece of writing, you have to understand that your ideas and interpretation will not be the same or maybe not even close to the interpretation of the people that read it. With that in mind, it really made me think through how I was going to word different sentences inside my paper so I was conveying the message I wanted. Although I believe I was able to show that I understood this concept in my papers, it may not have been the clearest because this was the first time that I had dealt with trying to understand different perspectives.

Another area that was sort of new to me was the modality within different forms of writing. I never really thought about multimodality, but there are at least two different types of modality in everything. This concept is always seen in marketing advertisements, and since I am a business major, it really appealed to me. The rhetorical triangle can also be applied to advertisements, so these topics had

Creel   5

me genuinely intrigued and I enjoyed learning about them. Ever since learning about the rhetorical triangle and other aspects, I have been applying that in a lot of the pieces I read and to all the advertisements I see. I think it is interesting because in most cases you can understand why advertisement companies did what they did on a commercial or billboard. On the other hand, there are some that leave you questioning the choices that were made, but you just know there was one reason or another.

Critical knowledge is the most important thing you can take away from this course because it is how you see yourself after the fifteen weeks. Looking back, I would have to say my second version of my Texts in Action is my best work because of the amount of understanding I gained. After I turned in my first paper, I realized that I did a lot of the paper wrong, so I received help and learned what areas were lacking. With that I was able to improve not only my writing, but also the concept. When I first wrote the paper, I was interpreting the article, not analyzing it. This led to many problems and at first I didn't understand why. After I had my "Ah-ha" moment, I felt that this piece of work was one of my best. My writing has improved so much over this course because now I understand *why* I am doing everything, rather than just knowing what I am doing. Everyone who has looked over my papers has helped me bring in that outside perspective and shown that not ev-

Creel   6

eryone thinks the way I do. I tend to get tunnel vision when I write papers. I think everyone understands what I am saying, but in reality I am the only one it makes sense to. If I had more time to fix my papers, I would definitely have more people read them because the more perspectives you get on something, the richer the feedback. One area that I need to continue to improve is my vocabulary. Whether or not I am sitting in an English class or a business class, I hear words that I have never heard but everyone else seems to know. Not only will this help me in life, but it can add a level of sophistication to my papers that I have never had before.

I have taken a lot away from this class that I will be able to use in all my work going forward. At first I was not super-excited to be taking an English class at night but I am very thankful I did. It was enjoyable and I got to explore a subject that I never really thought I liked, but in reality I enjoy being able to express my thoughts and improve my skills. It is crazy to think that this class is already over, but I know that everything I did will stay with me for a long time.

Thomas Dzierzak

Christiane Boehr

English Composition

1 December 2015

Reflection Essay

This class has taught me very much, not only about composition but about how I think and put my thoughts down on paper. At the beginning of the year, I really had no experience with using rhetoric or even what it was. As we learned about what it was, it became very easy to see it being used in our everyday lives. For example, commercials attempt to gain our trust through what companies want us to think are trustworthy sources, through playing on their audience's emotions, and through facts. It became increasingly apparent in articles that I read online and in print. Writing the Texts in Action helped me solidify this newfound knowledge of rhetoric by evaluating someone else's text. This assignment was tough for me in my first drafts, I ended up almost summarizing the article I was evaluating rather than actually evaluating. However, through the writing process and reading through my writing I was able to identify what I had messed up in the earlier drafts, teaching me to always read through my writing thoroughly. That way I make sure that I am actually writing what I need to be.

Dzierzak   2

Similar to rhetoric I did not have much previous knowledge about genre, audience, or purpose or really think about it too much. Through reading the assigned reading and lessons in class, I was able to identify genre, audience, and purpose. Then I was able to use my knowledge of genre, audience, and purpose to identify sources for my research paper. I was able to identify who the sources were directed towards, and then to direct my research paper toward the audience I want to speak to. This will help me to target my audience and write directly toward them, making my writing even stronger.

Things I had the most trouble with during this class were writing the Texts in Action and writing the research paper. As I discussed earlier I had difficulty keeping my end goal in focus. Luckily I was able to correct this mistake. From this, I really believe that I have improved my ability to hold my focus throughout my writing, and in the remainder of our composition assignments. I believe this is a skill that will continue to help me in the writing I will have to do later in my college journey, and in the various lab reports I will write in my engineering classes. The other assignment I had most trouble with most was the research paper. I had a difficult time extending my writing to reach the length desired. As I am a short-winded person and like to write things directly without explaining too much, not keeping in mind that my audience needs my ideas explained thoroughly. This forced me to

Dzierzak   3

dig deeper into my research and find even more evidence for the claims I make in my paper. Additionally, I had to find good excerpts of others' writing to include in my paper to help solidify my claims and prove them correct.

All in all, I have become a better writer being able to express my ideas thoroughly in my writing and through other mediums. The recast project was a great example of being able to express ideas through other mediums. I now believe that once you have mastered expressing ideas through words, it gets easier to express your ideas in other ways because you have even more resources to exemplify your idea through such as images, videos, and charts. These skills will help to make me a better engineer and businessman in the future. I will be able to share my thoughts and back them up solidly while being clear and to the point. I also think that I am better at presenting myself and having faith in myself, which is a necessity in the workplace. Without confidence, it will likely be very difficult to get a job since no one wants to hire someone who is not confident in himself. This confidence has grown through being confident in my ideas and my ability to share them. I am now much better at backing up my claims with factual evidence and other's ideas. I am confident in these abilities and cannot wait to share them with those I will work for and do business with in the future.

Howard

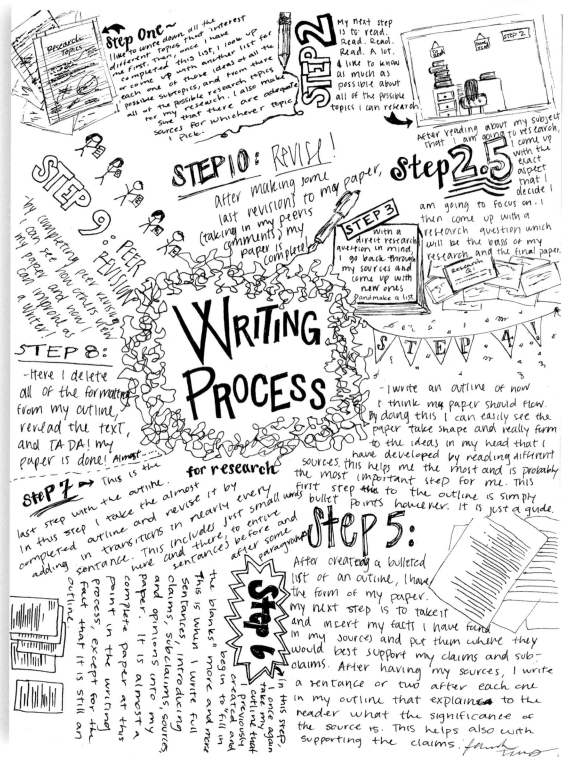

Step One~ I like to write down all the different topics that interest me first. Then, once I have completed this list, I look up or come up with another list for each one of those ideas of all the possible subtopics, and from there all of the possible research topics for my research. I also make sure that there are adequate sources for whichever topic I pick.

STEP 2 My next step is to read. Read. Read. Read. A lot. I like to know as much as possible about all of the possible topics I can research.

Step 2.5 After reading about my subject that I am going to research, I come up with the exact aspect that I decide I am going to focus on. I then come up with a research question which will be the basis of my research, and the final paper.

STEP 3 With a direct research question in mind, I go back through my sources and come up with new ones (and make a list.)

STEP 10: REVISE! After making some last revisions to my paper, (taking in my peer's comments) my paper is complete!

STEP 9: PEER REVISION By completing peer revision, I can see how others view my paper and now I can improve as a writer!

WRITING PROCESS
for research

STEP 4. -I write an outline of how I think my paper should flow. By doing this I can easily see the paper take shape and really form to the ideas in my head that I have developed by reading different sources. this helps me the most and is probably the most important step for me. This first step to the outline is simply bullet points however. It is just a guide.

STEP 8: -Here I delete all of the formatting from my outline, reread the text, and TA DA! my paper is done! Almost...

Step 7 → This is the last step with the outline. In this step I take the almost completed outline and revise it by adding in transitions in nearly every sentence. This includes just small words here and there, to entire sentences, before and after some paragraphs

Step 6 In this step, I once again take my outline that I previously created and begin to "fill in the blanks" more and more. This is when I write full sentences, introducing claims, subclaims, sources and opinions into my paper. It is almost a complete paper at this point in the writing process, except for the fact that it is still an outline.

Step 5: After creating a bulleted list of an outline, I have the form of my paper. My next step is to take it and insert my facts I have found in my sources and put them where they would best support my claims and sub-claims. After having my sources, I write a sentence or two after each one in my outline that explains to the reader what the significance of the source is. This helps also with supporting the claims.

Howard

Flyer courtesy Archives & Rare Books Library, University of Cincinnati.